Sedona Awakenings

Richard E. Carmen
Editor

Auricle Books
Sedona

Sedona Awakenings

Copyright 2013
Auricle Books

All rights reserved. No part of this book may be reproduced, stored in a retrieval system or transmitted in any form by any means electronic, mechanical, photocopying, recording or by other means without the written consent of the publisher.

10, 9, 8, 7, 6, 5, 4, 3, 2, 1
ISBN13 (Soft Cover): 978-0-9825785-4-4

Cover Development by Brad Peterson: www.BradPetersonArt.com
Cover photo and inside color photographic plates:
Jim Peterson, www.AspenHeightsImaging.com

Auricle Books
—an imprint of Auricle Ink Publishers—
P. O. Box 20607
Sedona AZ 86341
(928) 284-0860
www.BooksForHealingBodyMindAndSpirit.com

Contents

Preface		i

PART I: Introduction to Sedona

Chapter One	*Riding the Red Rock Wonderlands* **Joshua Placa**	3
Chapter Two	*They Say God Lives in Sedona* **Susan Obijiski**	9
Chapter Three	*Tour d'Sedona* **Dayna Lombardo**	13
Chapter Four	*A Really Good Friday* **Carol Gronewold**	19

PART II: Making the Quest

Chapter Five	*A Grand Canyon Nightmare* **Cheryl Sinn**	27
Chapter Six	*The Great Escape* **Pash Galbavy**	33
Chapter Seven	*A Spirit Quest* **Robin Lee Strom**	47

PART III: Dreams, Meditations and Visions

Chapter Eight	*Field of a Dream* **John Tamiazzo**	55
Chapter Nine	*The Birthday Party* **Miki Butterworth**	61
Chapter Ten	*The Mindful Teacher* **Richard E. Carmen**	67

PART IV: Signs, Voices and ETs

Chapter Eleven	*The Three Signs*	
	Chenoa Miller	83
Chapter Twelve	*The Labyrinth*	
	Janet Feeney	89
Chapter Thirteen	*The Encounter*	
	Kia Davenport	101

PART V: Love Stories

Chapter Fourteen	*A Love Story*	
	Karoline Grant	115
Chapter Fifteen	*Through The Fire*	
	Rose and Bryan Davis	123
Chapter Sixteen	*Flying High*	
	Karen Lombardi	131

PART VI: Death as a Teacher

Chapter Seventeen	*The Healer*	
	Shawn Bieber	137
Chapter Eighteen	*Free Fall*	
	Kristen M. Huard	141
Chapter Nineteen	*Journey of 10,000 Miles*	
	Loretta Jane Hido	147
Chapter Twenty	*Thelma and Louise*	
	Stacy Moore	153
Chapter Twenty-One	*Places in the Heart*	
	Sunny Schlenger	163

Sedona Awakenings

Sedona Awakenings

PREFACE
From the Editor

This book resulted from a writing competition Auricle Books sponsored May through July/2012. It was exclusively for present or past residents of Sedona who were invited to submit their true and intriguing stories about how they came to move here. There were three top winners First through Third Place with cash awards from $1000, $500 and $250 respectively. It was not known in May if this could actually evolve into a book. However, what became clear by June as the stories began streaming in was that there were some remarkable mysteries presented. Among the numerous submissions, in the end, these are the ones deemed worthy of publishing—some judged as interesting, some as fascinating, and some felt to be downright page-turning intrigue.

When I was about thirteen (around 1959), I happened to be watching television when an interview came on about the Maharishi Mahesh Yogi's first visit to America. He talked about how we all could reach our human potential through a simple technique called transcendental meditation—the ancient Vedic tradition of Enlightenment founded thousands of years ago in India. He spoke about the limitlessness of the mind and benefits of meditation, including a great inner sense of peace and relaxation that can lead to deeper thought and even finding *Self*. In essence, he was demonstrating how to use the body as a temple to the higher level of pure awareness—awakening the mind by quieting the thoughts. The idea intrigued me. The Maharishi chatted away and giggled innocently, explaining transcendental meditation while he eased himself comfortably into a full lotus position.

When the brief segment ended, I sat on the floor and wrapped my skinny legs into the same full lotus position, hoping for Enlightenment about which the Maharishi spoke. A deep awakening came swiftly. I was instantly overcome by the realization that if I remained in this position any longer my knee caps would snap off! I grabbed my legs like broken twisted sticks and with great dis-ease unencumbered my limbs back to their normal place on the floor.

And so goes Enlightenment and Awakening. You cannot force it. You cannot twist yourself into it. Perhaps the ancient art of rock-throwing known as the Runes has said it best, "You cannot push the river." Spirit must find its own flow within you, generally with tremendous preparation. Enlightenment is merely freedom from ignorance through the illumination of truth. Most often its absence comes at the expense of our Self. But true Enlightenment or Awakening as I've come to understand this is only discovered through the *inner world* by means of listening to our highest consciousness. Our ability to then apply such discoveries to the *outer world* becomes the very wisdom that not only benefits our Self, but potentially the world around us. Any good book is merely a signpost and guidance along a seeker's path to Awakening. In and of itself it does not awaken anyone. It is the person who must do the Awakening.

This is a theme you'll see repeated in various stories in this book. They reflect the writers' willingness to listen (*inner world wisdom*) and follow through on their instincts (*outer world benefits*). These writers said their stories were true. It was never my place or intention to challenge their truths. Therefore, these stories may be nothing more than a reflection of you and your own potential and perhaps how to listen more attentively. They might also represent your dreams and aspirations, your hopes and wishes. They were certainly watershed moments for these individuals who seem to clearly demonstrate that *when the student is ready the master appears* (in many forms).

I've also learned that the form in which Awakening comes is as unique as our fingerprints. Yet, chapter to chapter, common themes begin to rise off the pages. People have been drawn to Sedona in some of the most extraordinary ways. This book eases into the adventures first with background stories about Sedona so that you might better understand the later stories set in the context of quests, dreams, visions, voices, even death as stimulating forces. Many have come to find their lives almost manipulated through coincidences, synchronicities, even crazy rhythms that ultimately steered them to the heartbeat that is Sedona.

As you'll see, everyone was willing to drop their lives as they knew it, muster the courage and make the move. We do not yet really understand this higher driving force or why still others feel the beating pulse and are compelled to make the move. But what you'll find among these pages is that these explorers put on wings not knowing which way the wind would blow, and held steadfastly to their faith that the wind best knew where to take them.

And in so entrusting they found themselves *"Coming Home."*

—R. E. Carmen, Editor
Sedona, Arizona

Part I
Introduction to Sedona

"To look back to antiquity is one thing; to go back to it is another."
—Charles Caleb Colton (English cleric, writer and collector)

Sedona has a long history going back millions of years when it was just a seabed. Over millennia as the waters receded and nature carved the earth into mystical monuments, Sedona grew into its Sonoran desert landscape. It is estimated that the first Native Americans settled in this land about 10,000 years ago as pot makers and farmers. Many tribes over time have established themselves here, evidenced by prehistoric dwellings, ancient petroglyphs and ceramic artifacts. The Native Americans from this area have included the Paleo Indians (means *ancient ones*), Anasazi (*ancient ones who were not us*), Hopi (*humble and peaceful*), Hohokam (*those who have gone*), and Sinagua Indians (*without water*). It is known that there are parts of Sedona considered so sacred by the locals before white man came that no dwellings were built in these areas. They were used only for prayer, worship and ceremonies. Indeed, Sedona is something special. The sacredness of this land must surely represent that which is most sacred within ourselves. Thus, it should come as no surprise that the dwellers of this land would not only find their spiritual center in Sedona, but also within themselves. And so we too make the same journey.

There are prophecies among many Native American tribes that speak of a time in their future when great troubles will touch humanity. Mankind will be seduced and hearts that seek only understanding and compassion will reel in pain. It will be a time of great tumult that leads to the sacred gathering of people and return of the Sun God.

The future is now. The Gathering has begun.

CHAPTER ONE
Riding the Red Rock Wonderlands

 **Joshua Placa** freelances for national travel, motorcycle and adventure publications, and has contributed to major dailies. Whereabouts unknown, Placa is rumored to be holing up in a clapboard desert shack, chopper chained to his pet coyote, Stinky, and comfortably hiding from the Vatican. He is 56 and a resident of Sedona for eighteen years. Email joshua1@npgcable.com.

There had been tales of a charmed desert outpost, likely nothing more than urban legends and wishful thinking; spectacular landscapes sculpted by ancient earth-shaping forces and endless time—a place so moving it challenged empirical description. Something beyond the senses was tucked away within the sandstone folds of Sedona's crimson cliffs.

I had to reach beyond what could be seen to what could be felt by the legions that have made the crossing to these red rock wonderlands. Hearts rise to meet the rocky spires, standing like guardian sentinels over a land burnished with worn and weary souls.

I did not come to the New Age capital of Sedona for salvation or religion; nor was I guided by crystal nor psychic nor tarot or tantra. I was not drawn by promises of pure love or enlightenment, but by something else, something more primal.

I crossed the Hudson and left the hive behind. The frenetic metropolis had lost its hum, it's once booming concrete canyons falling quiet. Time to find a new place to dwell, so I loaded up the Harley with all it could carry and turned its front wheel west, seeking friendlier climes and undiscovered country. Moving to Sedona felt like I was changing planets.

There are a few, rare destinations on the paved side of the planet that can be considered true meccas for motorcyclists. One worth the pilgrimage is a place possessing almost supernatural beauty. If I ever questioned why

I ride, Sedona offers an epiphany. It is a dazzling moment that brings the passion and poetry of my leathery life into crystal clarity.

This is where nature has preserved some of its greatest works. The landscape appears unchanged since dinosaurs ruled the Permian plains, eons before the earliest hominid creatures could dream of pink jeeps and full-moon drum circles. Everything in this desert wants to bite, prick, sting or devour you, yet I felt invited in and welcomed. Sedona drew me to its side, a wayward biker in search of little more than fresh adventure and the next cold beer, joining me to these haunting hills and naked horizons.

Imagination feels reborn in a place like this. Shadows turn to shapes and come alive. In Sedona, the surreal becomes real, filling the unearthly rock formations with something fantastic. It's not hard to spot a dinosaur on occasion or other such cryptozoological creature as I turn a curve or ride into a glaring sunset, only to see giant shadows bound into the wilderness. Riding through it feels like wandering around another epoch, a fanciful trip into a H. G. Wells novel.

This whimsical town two hours north of Phoenix is a biker's paradise, a sacred place where road, climate and scenery converge to create an unparalleled Eden for man and motorcyclist alike. Inland Jurassic seas invaded and retreated, cycling over millions of years to deposit the sand, mud and lime that would become Sedona's signature buttes and mesas. Deposits rich in iron created the various shades of red, rusting through the brittle rock. Unnoticed by most visitors, a few extinct volcanoes hide in the shadows of the older sedimentary rock.

Sedona is host to no fewer than five energy vortices, rock formations thought to emit spiritual energy and claimed by true believers to be portals to other dimensions, and when the stars and planets align, one-way passage to the mother ship. But seeing the weather- and wind-sculpted rock can offer a different kind of spiritual experience. For me, the best vantage point was aboard two wheels, where instincts, awareness and senses are heightened and a connection felt when the earth rolls out naked before you, revealing curves and shapes before unexposed.

The rocks seem to shift in color from dawn to dusk, appearing red, orange or pink, offering an almost impressionist perspective of the wonder around us. Seasonal monsoons rumble in from July through September, marked by high winds, pelting rain and hail, and sometimes led by a howling wall of dust and lightning. Legend has it that on some dark days it's not a storm, but the Devil himself chasing your soul.

Sedona has attracted generations of Native Americans, artists, ranchers, mountain bikers, hikers, moviemakers, some aliens, New World Order advance guards, a few wayward bikers, and anyone in search of new faith and healing. Reportedly, some 3.3 million tourists per year visit Sedona, second in the state to only the Grand Canyon.

Some 10,000 people live here, not counting inter-dimensional creatures of various natures and intents, angels, devils, witches, a smattering of hell-raisers and even, by some accounts, a lost desert tribe of Bigfoots. At some point or another, all have been reported seen about town. But the real attraction to Sedona is simply being here, riding the smooth black ribbons that wrap around the blood-red stone.

The spellbinding area offers some of the best motorcycling on this planet, or any other planet. Perhaps the most scenic 10-mile stretch in the world begins just north of town on Highway 89A. Oak Creek cut a canyon from the Mogollon Rim, an unexplained abrupt rise in solid rock traveling hundreds of miles across northern Arizona, south into Sedona, leaving towering bluffs to cradle the valley below.

The road clings to Oak Creek, passing Slide Rock State Park, a popular swimming spot noted for its smooth, waterslide-like flat red rocks; West Fork, one of the most beautiful hiking trails found anywhere, and a few more spots to shop if you're so inclined. There are many points along the way to pull over and hike in and around the canyon, or take a short walk down to the creek. It's hard not to continuously crane your neck, trying to take in one impressive sight after another as you roll by immense petrified ocean reefs that tower over the pine, aspen and juniper trees below.

It's difficult to ride a block in this town without passing a crystal or tarot card shop, palm reader, bead boutique, massage therapist, psychic healer and various and sundry shops selling western wear, Navajo and Hopi jewelry, T-shirts and assorted knickknacks. Sometimes forgotten by locals is Sedona's standing as a world-class artist colony, boasting some of the country's finest galleries. The work is predominantly western and Native American, providing a rare glimpse into desert culture.

At the northern end of town sits a great cluster of stores hawking the predictable tourist detritus, and some things not so expected, such as restaurants serving buffalo and rattlesnake, as well as shops like the Cowboy Corral, which can outfit a tinhorn in authentic 1880s garb and gear. My closet and Old West alter ego are filled with the stuff. Jeep and Hummer tours, horseback riding, mountain biking, ATV, helicopter, balloon and vintage plane rides round out the recreation.

Tuzigoot National Monument, about 30 minutes west of Sedona in Clarkdale gives us a sense of our shared hunter/gatherer past, a memory somehow locked in our DNA. The Sinagua Indian pueblo is set in a river basin nearly unchanged since its 110 rooms bustled with a great village, a hub comparable to a major modern city in relative size and activity.

Tuzigoot was home to more than 300 people at its peak when most villages were small, self-sufficient clans of ten or twenty. It was inhabited from approximately 1,000-1,400 AD when the Sinagua mysteriously vanished. About forty minutes southeast of Sedona in Camp Verde is Montezuma's Castle, a 50-room, restored pueblo built beneath a sprawling limestone overhang. The fallow fields below were thought to be once thriving with cultivated corn and legumes. The Verde River flowed just beyond the fields making it an ideal location for a settlement, one that endured some four-hundred years, coincidentally about the same age as the city I left.

Theories abound regarding the disappearance of tribal peoples from the area. No evidence of epidemic or mass violence has surfaced, prompting explanations ranging from absorption into larger or invading tribes to critical loss of bio diversity to alien abduction. Anthropologists tend to agree the most likely cause was years of extended drought eventually forced villagers to abandon their ancestral homes and seek more fruitful territories. Sometimes, the frenetic metropolis loses its hum, the canyons fall quiet and it's time to find a friendlier place to dwell.

CHAPTER TWO
They Say God Lives in Sedona

Susan Obijiski is a business writer, author, business consultant, Reiki Master, holistic practitioner and teacher. Her novel, *Dreams of the Many,* is about shared humanity and a reminder of our capacity to overcome fears and become what we were meant to be. Susan is 61 and a resident of Sedona for six years. [www.susanobijiski.com/dreams_of_the_many.htm]

Someone once said, "God made the Grand Canyon, but she lives in Sedona." If you've seen the red rocks of Sedona, you know that is true. For us, the journey began with a trip from New York to Tucson to attend the annual Gem and Mineral Show. After attending the event, we had a few extra days of vacation. We heard that Sedona was filled with fake psychics, fringe lunatics and snake oil salesman, and we really weren't interested in that experience. In spite of our misgivings, we decided to see what all the fuss was about. I am not sure why!

We drove up Interstate-17 and took the Sedona exit onto Route 179 to begin our Sedona journey. There is a point on this road—Sedona and Oak Creek residents are very familiar with this spot—where you round a bend and see the red rocks for the first time. Bell Rock and Courthouse Butte stand majestically against the backdrop of a pristine blue sky as they have for centuries beyond reckoning. This is the place where many tourists forget that there is traffic behind them. They stop their cars in the middle of the road to take a picture. It is a breathtaking view!

We arrived at our hotel in the Village of Oak Creek and went to bed, exhausted from travel. When we awoke, we walked out onto the balcony and found ourselves staring at Bell Rock. There it was; so close we could almost touch it. We spent our days hiking, and visited a vortex or two, as do many tourists who come to this paradise.

The tribal residents of the area do not include energy vortexes in their legends, but they do respect and honor this beautiful land, and it is sacred to them, as it is to those of us who now share this land with them. For us, the vortex energy was real, and the canyons of red rock were awe inspiring. Some people are attracted to Sedona because of its undeniable beauty and some because it nourishes their soul. No matter why you decided to make this journey, it all comes down to the same thing. The staggering beauty and ancient serenity of the red rocks is life-changing.

On the last day of our vacation, we got in the car to drive back to the airport. My husband made an unscheduled stop at the office of a local realtor. He picked up a listing of homes for sale and told the realtor that he was interested in buying land. We had not talked about it, and yet his inquiry seemed right. As it happened a piece of land came on the market the very next day and the realtor sent us pictures. Within a month, we returned to Sedona to see the property. There were minor glitches along the way, but the move seemed to be our destiny and every obstacle was quickly overcome. It was simply meant to be!

We have been in Sedona for nearly six years and the adventure has been inspiring and fulfilling. I have heard stories about people visiting Sedona and never leaving. Apparently, the draw was so irresistible that they didn't go home to sell the house or to pack belongings. They simply stayed!

It is true that Sedona attracts all kinds of people. Some of our residents are quirky and unusual. Some come to Sedona to become gurus, or preach their special brand of spirituality with the expectation of making a million dollars. Many of us ignore the trappings of the tourist experience, choosing instead to remain grounded in the beauty and the energy that surround us. I believe that the gospel of Sedona is much simpler than the lessons taught by our modern day gurus. These lessons are found in the land and in the fabric of nurturing energy that flows through every canyon and surrounds every red rock spire. All you have to do is close your eyes and feel the lessons the earth has to offer. Live each day, surrounded by the beauty and magnificence of this magical place—regardless of your religious or spiritual beliefs.

As Sedona residents we have the privilege of sharing that gift with visitors, friends, and neighbors. Sedona means something different to every person and its gifts are given, based on what each person needs. Whether you come for the vortex energy or the uplifting beauty of the natural surroundings, Sedona will touch your heart and nourish your soul. It will change you in ways you cannot imagine. It's true what they say. God really does live in Sedona!

CHAPTER THREE
Tour d'Sedona

Dayna Lombardo was born in Los Angeles and raised in North Miami Beach, Florida, and has a 20 year-old son, Alex. She has pursued a career as a Radiology Technologist for the past thirty years and enjoys all watersports, hiking, exploring, writing, music and dabbles with photography and art. Dayna is 53 and has lived in Sedona for about two years.

As I entered Red Rock Country I was in awe. The massive red rock formations seemed non-stop. Each was more beautiful than the next. The turquoise blue sky, puffy white clouds and wildflowers—it was like a painting, so surreal. In my amazement I paused everywhere I looked. I saw God. Not literally of course, but it was so clear that this had been created by a master artist. Sedona is definitely where God shows off! Just when I thought it could not get better, it did, over and over again. I could put no names to the formations. They were just massive red mountains.

I began to imagine what this incredible place was like years ago, before the concrete, the hotels and the roundabouts. I saw wide open ranges with cattle and horses, cowboys, saloons and stagecoaches. An old western movie played in my mind. I imagined Native Americans living their visions on this beautiful land. My mind raced with thoughts of just how wonderful it must have been to be here then.

As I drove on, I realized I was in the Village of Oak Creek and had not even reached Sedona yet. Redness surrounded me as the road wound its way through this magical area.

My exploration of these wonders continued for the next three hours. Uptown with its quaint, contemporary stores, galleries and restaurants was the beginning of the scenic ride up Oak Creek Canyon to Midgley Bridge. I parked my car and stepped out onto this sacred land and shot photo after photo from all angles, zooming in on the faces I began to see in the rocks. Never before had I felt such peace and joy. For me, this was heaven. God's country.

I headed back toward Uptown, swerving round the roundabouts and up the hill into West Sedona. There I saw that people really do live here and work here. The red rocks towered over beautiful houses on hills and appeared to be never-ending. The wind and 'click-click-click' of my camera was all I heard as I drove along in total amazement.

I checked into my hotel located on Thunder Mountain ('Grayback Mountain' before they changed the name). I picked up a book at the front desk written by a local woman. How cool! I put my suitcase in my room and wandered out into the beauty. I walked and walked for hours taking photos. The sun began to change the color of the rocks and in spots they were suddenly bright yellow, pink and orange. I'd never seen anything like this. My first Sedona sunset was pure magic. I was out somewhere close to Thunder Mountain as the sky turned bright pink and quickly shades of purple, the most magnificent colors I'd ever seen. Ravens passed silently through the sky and bats dipped into the vastness. It was so quiet. So peaceful and serene.

Walking back to my hotel I felt so blessed to be in this magical land. Lying on my bed I stared at the photos taken earlier, over and over again, and could hardly wait for the sun to rise so I could experience more.

Upon waking, I took my coffee and sat outside on the balcony and knew *I am home.* Another beautiful day in paradise was about to begin. As I ventured down Dry Creek Road into Boynton Canyon, I passed Lizard Rock, Chimney Rock and drove deep into the canyon where the presence of the Native American was felt so strongly. On this day I wanted to see where they had lived and was on my way to Palatki and Honanki. I was excited.

The drive out was breathtaking and riding on the dirt road made my adventure seem like it may have been in days past. First to Palatki, where I learned of the Sinagua—the people of the Red Rocks. Sinagua means without water. That may be why they left their home. I stood in Red Canyon and saw the dwellings built long ago, which are still upheld, and I wondered how they stayed intact over the years. On to the pictographs and I was in a place of peace. I felt the presence of the Sinagua. It was unexplainable. I wanted more.

I ventured further out to Honanki where there were more dwellings and pictographs. I was warned that a rattlesnake had been sited and was reminded that this is their territory. Fearless, I began my uphill journey. I saw a tree with alligator bark and forest-like beauty. Then, there they were, the beautiful dwellings. Some had crumbled over the years, but parts were still intact. The ranger on duty was very informative and pointed to the handprints on the walls as well as the pictographs and petroglyphs. I felt so lucky to be there, to experience this wonder and to feel the peace and presence of the past. Photos in my brain as well as on my camera will never let me forget where I was, and the history that spoke without language.

I wished I could have been here back then, when there was nothing here, only nature. I drove back to civilization in a state of bliss. I relived over and over in my mind what I had just experienced. Back on the pavement I drove up to the Aerie lookout that has since become one of my favorite places to watch the sunset.

I drove all over the canyon, stopping to take pictures, to get lost in the beauty and to see more. My ride back up was so tranquil. I knew there was so much more to experience. I drove up and down the streets of West Sedona catching each red rock at every possible angle, gazing at the landscapes of cactus and rocks. This was so unlike Florida the place I called home. Again, my camera clicked away. How could any place be so magnificent?

On 89A I headed east and up to the Airport Mesa. Cruising up this steep hill it was hard to keep my eyes on the road because rock formations were everywhere and I had to catch them. As I reached the mesa (elevation over 4,800 feet), I headed to the overlook and took photos that probably every person who has ever visited Sedona has taken. Breathtaking! The mesa was filling up with tourists like me. The sun was about to set in beautiful Sedona. The lookout was full and tripods as well as telephoto lenses were ready to catch this spectacular daily event. The colors on this night were red and orange. Covering the fluffy clouds the color-filled sky changed its many contrasts of shades on the red rocks. Many writers have written about this same moment, yet, descriptions still escaped me.

Dinner on the terrace of Wildflower Bakery in the Hyatt Plaza was made so comfortable with a slight breeze. Rock figures were everywhere. Snoopy was in perfect sight and Woodstock stood on his nose. You didn't need an imagination to see these images represented in the red rocks. Amazing! The food was great—salmon Caesar salad with fresh baked bread. I window shopped, then headed back to the hotel. High in the sky there was a bright white cross over the darkening mountain. This place is so cool! Another spirit-filled day in Sedona had come to an end. What would tomorrow bring I wondered?

A new day was to bring a private tour with the local who wrote the book. She arrived in her minivan and off we went to explore. We headed back down into Boynton Canyon to a place I may never find again. It was a lookout. She took pictures of my back while I sat on a large rock looking out to the horizon. She told me this is very spiritual. She was right. I now love to photograph people from behind.

Off to the Kachina Woman. She was a Hopi woman rock formation that is supposed to watch over the women of Sedona. We hiked up to a vista and sat with this amazing form. Someone in the canyon was playing a flute. The wind picked up. My local guide sang a spiritual prayer as the wind blew and the temperature dropped. Again I sensed the presence of long ago and the Hopi people on the land. I love this place. The hike back down was invigorating as we anticipated Red Rock State Park next. We passed the high school and up we went to the most magnificent sights, then down and into the park.

We walked along the creek and took lots of pictures. We spoke about our lives and I shared my long story of the past year of my life, about my mother becoming very sick and dying in my home, the break-up of a three-year relationship, and my only child going away to college. I told her about my job and how I felt as though the time had come to move on. She shared with me certain things about her life and we bonded as women.

Along the way she educated me on the names of the plants, trees and flowers. We picked up cotton bits, rocks, twigs and wild flowers. I had no idea what I was about to encounter—a vortex—Cathedral Rock at Red Rock Crossing. Another moment.

We sat down on the flat rock surface leading to the creek. We made a boat with all of the pieces of nature we had gathered. Together we said a prayer to let go of the past and set our little boat onto the water. It slowly sailed away. Freedom! My past fears, guilt and insecurities were in that little boat—gone forever I was hoping.

We walked further into the woods and there it was, Buddha Beach. Thousands of rocks set on top of rocks everywhere! People from all over the world helped to make this special place. Still today I love Buddha Beach.

The hike back to the minivan was fun. Something had changed in me. I was at peace with myself and I felt great. After being dropped off at my hotel I quickly took my car east again and headed back to the Village of Oak Creek where Bell, Courthouse and Castle Rock were waiting to be explored. The scenic drive on Highway 179 passed Cathedral Rock from the other side, Elephant Rock and the beautiful Chapel built right into the red rocks. I hiked the seven miles around Bell and Courthouse identifying the plants, flowers and trees that I had learned about earlier in the day. Bell Rock is a vortex too and the energy from that powerful red rock formation created peace inside my being. With red dust on my sandals, I was ready to call it a day. From the parking lot the view was clear of the hot Sedona sun setting over the red rocks once again. This night was my favorite— powerful pink.

In the morning I was on the hotel computer and typed my résumé along with a letter of resignation. *I am moving to Sedona!* Six weeks later I drove cross country with my son and arrived at my new residence, ready to start my new job and new life in Sedona. Who'd have thought?

POSTSCRIPT: My job is great. I have the opportunity to help people, just as in Florida, and meet people experiencing Sedona from all over the world. I get to share my experiences, show photos and guide them where to go and what to see. On my days off I continue to explore the land, hiking and climbing these beautiful formations. My first week here a beautiful mountain lion passed through my backyard. Bobcats, javelina, rabbits, quail, woodpeckers, hummingbirds, ravens and deer are everywhere. The creek has become my ocean and hiking the hidden ruins and dwellings are my passion. My favorite places for meditation, quiet and peace are deep in the red rocks of Sedona.

CHAPTER FOUR
A Really Good Friday

Carol Gronewold lives a contented life of variety including being a housewife, mom to her two dogs, and secretary for her husband's construction business (Gronewold Construction). Her favorite personal achievement: she followed her bliss by creating a hand-lettered, illustrated cookbook, *The Secret Recipe* (self-published, 2010). Carol is 60 and has lived in Sedona for twenty-seven years. [www.TheSecretRecipeCookbook.com]

Each time I reflect on the day we discovered Sedona I feel as if it was yesterday. Driving westward on Interstate 40, on a February day, 1985, brilliant snow-capped mountains of the San Francisco Peaks appeared out of nowhere. What an awesome sight! At the same moment, we were being serenaded by the famous song, *America the Beautiful,* playing on our pickup's radio. My husband Loren and I did not speak a word as we intently listened to every word of that song as it intermingled with the wondrous view. It was thrilling. I felt I was in a trance. Nothing like this had ever happened to us. At last, Loren and I gazed at each other commenting on how unusual it was hearing that song at noon on a weekday. And then to have it coincide with such a picturesque view! As I think back on that day I'm positive we were being guided into our lives as we know them today, some twenty-seven years later.

We stopped in Flagstaff for lunch. Waiting for food to arrive at our restaurant table, I glanced at a map to see how far away we were from a good-sized town by the Interstate where we could stay that night. As I was 'scouting the map, the name Sedona popped out at me like a Bingo number being called. Instantly I felt a sense of adventuresome excitement.

I asked Loren, "Remember a month ago when the television program *Portrait of America* was about Arizona?"

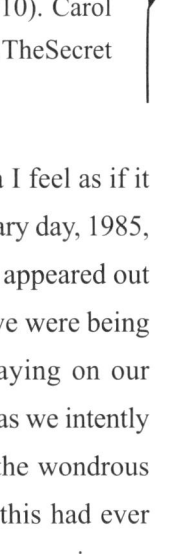

"Yes," he confirmed, with a very inquisitive look on his face.

"Weren't we fascinated with a little town called Sedona?"

"Yes, I think so. Why?"

"Well, it's only 30 miles away and I think we should take a little side trip and check it out. We have a couple hours to spare. I'd really like to see it."

He wholeheartedly agreed.

Loren and I are from Gothenburg, Nebraska, a 3,000 resident small-town farming community. Even though we were both born and raised there we had an intense yearning to relocate when the farming economy soured in the early 80s. Loren's construction jobs became few and far between. I managed to find or create a variety of jobs that at least paid enough for food and some of the bills. Our mortgage was only $275 a month and we really struggled coming up with the money for it. We are both very creative individuals and we felt so stifled and stuck in a rut. We knew the only way out was to move. Where? We hadn't a clue. We checked out a few places, but nothing felt right.

Our luck changed when Loren's cousin in California called, asking if we would be interested in coming there to remodel his kitchen. The only drawback we had was our 'cash on hand' situation. He sent us enough money for gas so we could drive to his place. We readily accepted. It was an offer we couldn't refuse. We packed necessary tools for the job and enough clothes to get us through the month it would take to complete the work. A friend would stay at our house to take care of our pets. We were on our way to unknown territory. It was an opportunity to explore the countryside as we traveled.

After we finished our lunch we drove down the curving, winding Highway 89A toward Sedona. The thickly forested area outside Flagstaff was beautiful, but each corner we rounded and every step-down in elevation brought new breathtaking sights. I will never forget—and I mean *never*—the sight of those glorious magnificent red rocks as we drove around each bend coming closer to the mysterious, intriguing town we were seeking. I felt magnetism drawing the center of my soul onward. I hadn't ever experienced anything like it. I didn't want it to end. If this was the appetizer, what would be the main street entrée?

The closer we got to Sedona I kept wondering, what's coming next? It couldn't get much better. But it did. We began traveling through uptown Sedona witnessing many tourist shops in the quaint area. In our hometown of Gothenburg, there was only one tourist attraction, an original Pony Express Station. Sedona's attractions were so intriguing, I was anxious to see more.

We drove through a few residential and commercial areas before we parked our truck in the large parking lot of the new tourist shopping complex, Tlaquepaque. When we got out of the truck I glanced around noticing limousines, Cadillacs, gold-plated license plates and many out-of-state license plates on new vehicles. I remember feeling a little out of place with our older Dodge pickup loaded with its construction lumber racks and the plywood-covered bed concealing Loren's construction tools. I did, however, feel very proud of myself when I realized I had correctly pronounced *T-lah-ka-pa'-kee* the first time I spoke it.

We only had about another hour to spare before we had to get back on the road so we decided to browse a couple art galleries. As we were walking from one gallery to another I tried to contain my adrenaline-induced thoughts as I declared to Loren, "I know this may sound strange, but all at once I feel like we have found home."

He has never been one to make rash decisions, but with little hesitation he agreed. That was our awakening to realize our California job was the ticket we needed to make enough extra money to move to Sedona. We left Sedona that afternoon with a new song in our hearts, 'Sedona, the Beautiful.'

The entire month we were in Los Angeles we kept dreaming of Sedona, knowing it was right for us. We completed the remodel and at the end of March drove back to Sedona on our way to Nebraska. Sedona was just as magical as we had remembered. We spent one night in a local motel. The next day we talked with a couple rental agencies. By following intuitive positive instincts, we took the plunge and rented a suitable house. We had enough cash saved to pay first and last month's rent. We were confident we would find work once we moved.

It was Friday. It was Good Friday. And it really was a good Friday! Sunday would be Easter and both of our families would be at each of our parent's homes for the holiday weekend. If we drove all night we could get there and make our 'moving' announcement to everyone. We had never driven that long before, but we were so excited we knew we could do it. By the light of a full moon that night, I know we were kept safe, alert, and guided by God. We drove 1,000 miles from Friday evening until the afternoon on Saturday. Our only stops were for gas, bathroom breaks, a quick meal at a gas station, and an hour of brief napping while sitting in the truck at an Interstate rest stop. We spent Easter with both of our families and told them the news. They were happy for us, but sad we were leaving.

We had an auction of a good part of our household items, put our home on the market, said our goodbyes. Loren drove a fully loaded U-Haul truck, towing his pickup behind. I drove my car. Cats aren't good travelers, but I had three of our disgruntled characters with me. Loren had our sweetheart basset hound, Ginny, as his traveling companion. On May 1, 1985, we arrived in Sedona.

POSTSCRIPT: The second day while we were moving into our rental home, Loren got a job with a local contractor. I began working as a companion for an older couple two weeks later. Loren now has his own construction business and I have done a wide variety of work and creativity over the years. We're not rich as far as money goes, but we feel rich in so many other ways. We truly appreciate opportunities that have come to us. Sedona has treated us well. On bad days, all we have to do is step outside and look at the spectacular red rock surroundings. On good days, which there have been more than the bad, Loren and I remind each other how very fortunate we are to be so blessed living here. Sedona has gifted us with so many wonderful friends, neighbors and acquaintances. Everyone we meet has a different story about where they are from and how they arrived here. We're all here for the same reason. I believe God closes one door to open another. We're home.

Part II
Making the Quest

"Not all those who wander are lost."
—J.R.R. Tolkien, *Fellowship of the Ring*

Sometimes the unpredictability of life throws us onto a path we never saw coming, which can challenge us in the process of unraveling its mystery. However, like knights-errant in medieval times, we may be driven by a force deep within for pure survival or for pure truth. Either way, it's a journey.

CHAPTER FIVE
A Grand Canyon Nightmare

Cheryl Sinn was the Second Place Winner with the following essay submitted to the Mystical Sedona Stories Writing Contest.® She was born a gifted artist and raised in Philadelphia until the age of 22. She enjoys art, traveling, the outdoors, animals, spirituality and spending time with friends. Cheryl is married and currently works as the Business Manager at the Sedona Arts Center. She's 50 and has lived in Sedona for twenty-eight years.

I was 22 years old in 1984 when I put a backpack on for the very first time. I was born and raised in Philadelphia, but always knew I belonged somewhere else. Traveling was in my blood and so was the West. As a teenager I wore feather earrings and cowboy boots to the Creative and Performing Arts High School in the city.

That year I made the life changing decision to hitchhike around the USA searching for the perfect place to live. My journey lasted a couple months and took me from the East to the West Coast and back again, but it was Mother Nature and the Grand Canyon that changed my life forever.

The backpack I was carrying weighed about 50 pounds and was filled with all the items a 22 year-old girl could need traveling from city to country to city to national parks inclusive of one mini-skirt and one pair of high heels. I slept in a hostel in Flagstaff and the next morning stashed half of the items from my pack into a bus locker at the local Nava-Hopi Bus Depot. My plan was to hike the Grand Canyon . . . a natural wonder of the world.

When I arrived at the Canyon around July 25th, I was very surprised to see signs and streets and rules. It took me four days of living on the South Rim to obtain the permits necessary to go into the Canyon and stay overnight at Phantom Ranch. I had it all mapped out—Bright Angel trail to Indian Gardens campground to Phantom for a couple nights and back up a different trail. It was going to be a feat of endurance both mentally and physically for this city slicker, and I was ready to face it head-on by myself!

I started my descent early in the morning that hot August day with lots of water, trail mix and instant meals. It was amazing for the first couple of miles and then it started to rain. I had no idea what a monsoon was so I enjoyed the cooling of the water. As I continued, so did the rain. It began raining harder and harder and all the people below me on the trail started leaving, passing me by on their way back to the Rim. I had waited too long and come too far to let a little rain dampen my spirit or my plans so I continued walking.

I trudged along until I couldn't see the trail. Torrential rains were creating mud smoke so thick that I couldn't see my own hand in front of my eyes. Hail hit me in the face and then lightning and thunder began. I thought . . . *this can't be good! I'm wearing an aluminum backpack! Maybe my rubber sneakers will stop me from being struck by lightning?* Heart pounding now I found refuge under a big boulder figuring I'd wait out the storm. Little did I know it had just begun.

Once under the rocks, the earth started to shake and lightning bolts came so close I think they were bouncing off of my boulder. That's when I started to pray, but Mother Nature had other plans and the trail started to move and the avalanche began. Boulders and mud started sliding down the mountain and over my head—boulders the size of a Volkswagen bug! Even as I write these words twenty-eight years later, my heart pounds in my chest reliving the terrifying minutes. I took my journal out of my pack and began to record what I thought was my last day on earth. The action of writing while under the boulder wasn't for purposes of keeping a record, but more of a letting out of my emotions. It turned out to be just a bunch of wet scribble to anyone else trying to read it! I wrote and cried and prayed for at least half an hour by which time the storm subsided. As the air began to clear I pinched myself to make sure I was still alive and took a deep breath.

Just as I was gaining composure a loud voice shouted, "Hey YOU! What are you doing down there?" I crawled out of my hiding space to find a ranger above me on another boulder. He looked at me and said, "Get up here, the floods are coming down!" My mind was thinking—*floods? What floods? I thought that already happened!*

I scrambled up to his perch just in time to watch the Bright Angel trail be engulfed by a raging river, just before the first rush of it reached my boots. All of the storm water that had accumulated at the top was now reaching our position. I watched in complete disbelief as the trail was washed away completely. The ranger and I talked for fifteen minutes about monsoons and then he said that it was safe for me to start back up the trail to the top now.

I explained, "But I'm not heading up, sir. I'm on my way down now that the storm is over."

We basically argued for a few minutes until he said that he couldn't force me to leave. Blood rushing, heart pounding, head reeling, adrenaline coursing through me, I was on my way back down.

Bright Angel Trail wasn't really a trail anymore. More of a meandering wash of rocks and boulders instead. As I walked I thanked God to be alive and tried to shake off the shock of what I had just experienced. I must have walked for another half mile when I came upon two men stopped in front of a river of water preventing them from going any farther. Steve and Huntar from Sedona had also gotten caught in the flash floods and were waiting out the storm. I was so delighted to see other hikers I started blurting out all of my emotions and screaming, "The wooder! The wooder!" I was talking so fast and so hard I didn't realize they had no idea what I was saying. My East Coast accent made my shrieks about 'water' sound like a foreign language.

Steve and Huntar were taking a trip to the Canyon to camp for the weekend. Life threatening experiences can cause immediate connections and understandings and that's what happened to the three of us. As we each took turns sharing our internal fears, shock and emotions of what just happened, we became brothers and sister. We decided to continue our journey together. They also had permits to go to Indian Gardens and then Phantom Ranch. It seemed natural to join them for the rest of the journey. The river in front of us eventually slowed enough to allow us to get to the other side and make it to Indian Gardens.

Indian Gardens Campsite had been destroyed so there were no real campsites to speak of, but we each set up our tents for the evening in whatever dry spots we found. We continued to get to know each other and hiked to Pinnacle Point for the awesome 2000 foot overlook into the Colorado River. We ate dinner together and after such an emotional adventure, hit the sack early.

I was sound asleep when I felt like I was floating. It was pitch dark so I couldn't actually see the water rambling under my tent, but I could hear the rain. At the same time, a siren so deafening sounded and another ranger appeared in the dark yelling at us to get up higher, "The floods are coming again!" Steve, Huntar and I climbed trees for safety and started praying again. When the rain subsided to drizzle and by the early morning light we saw that our tents and most of our gear had washed away. We knew then it was time to get the hell out of the Canyon!

The climb out was agonizing. What should have taken four hours took us nine. The trail was now nothing but boulders. City slicker turned mountain rock climber in a day! Steve in front of me and Huntar behind me was the only reason I was ever able to make it out that day, instructing me one step at a time, moment by moment. The rain never really stopped all day and by the time we got to the top we were exhausted and inseparable! Unbeknownst to us, people at the rim were aware of our plight and expecting us. We were taken to Bright Angel Lodge where we ate and collapsed for the night. I remember having to go to the bathroom in the middle of the night and staggering out of bed and falling flat on my face because my leg muscles were useless. We all laughed ourselves back to sleep.

In the morning, I asked the boys to drive me back to Flagstaff to pick up the rest of my belongings at the bus station. They said only if I came back to Sedona with them. At first I refused stating I wanted to get the heck out of Arizona and make my way to California. But they were relentless and refused to take me to Flagstaff unless I promised to go home with them. So we loaded into that magnificent CJ7 Jeep with roll bars and let the wind hit our faces and began our next journey while recalling our story over and over again.

Steve drove the back roads through the little Colorado and Indian lands. We stopped at the Navajo vendor's selling their jewelry, took side trips, and ate lunch all before arriving in Flagstaff. After picking up my belongings we headed south to find a weird-named dirt path—Schnebly Hill Road. Steve told me this was the route that the original pioneers and cattle used to travel to and from Flagstaff to Sedona. The drive was the most energizing, fun and liberating feeling as I hung onto the roll bars bouncing through the open meadows and back woods of Coconino National Forest, mile by mile getting closer and closer to the edge of the Mogollon Rim. There was no possible way for Steve or Huntar to prepare me for what I was about to see when we arrived at the top of Schnebly Hill Road overlooking Sedona. It was breathtaking. I knew instantly I was home.

During the next two weeks I explored the Verde Valley by jeep and foot. The boys were the best guides and shared their life and their friends. We watched the sun set on top of Sugarloaf Mountain when you could still 4-wheel to the top, hung out in the creek at Dutchman's Cove when Hawkeye RV Park was still open to the public, hiked through Boynton

Canyon before Enchantment existed and at the end of each sun-drenched hot day, we cooled off with a cold beverage at the local hangout and swinging door saloon, the Oak Creek Tavern.

I fell in love with the small town and the blend of artists, bikers, Indians and Cowboys. I fell in love with the community of uptown and the freedom to sell artwork on the sidewalks to travelers finding their own way to the Grand Canyon. And best of all, everyone knew their neighbor by name, and I was now one of them.

I made up my mind Sedona would be my home, but I still had an apartment in Philadelphia. I continued my journey traveling up and down the West Coast for a month and returned to Sedona for a week before flying back to Philadelphia. I made a promise to myself and my new friends that I would return as soon as possible.

Over the next eight months I worked constantly to earn as much money as I could, and every Saturday night I called the Oak Creek Tavern and talked to Steve, Huntar and the many other locals I had met so as not to lose my dream. In June of 1985 I bought a car, sold everything that could not fit in it, and drove the 2,500 miles back to Sedona. I've been here ever since.

POSTSCRIPT: The boys (now men) and I remain friends in town and in heart. Sadly, Huntar died a few years ago, but Steve is married with kids and lives in Cottonwood. I kept my connection to the artist in me and to the uptown I fell in love with, and currently am the Business Manager for the Sedona Arts Center.

In loving memory of Huntar Grove.

CHAPTER SIX
The Great Escape

Pash Galbavy, M.A., was the First Place Winner with the following essay submitted to the Mystical Sedona Stories Writing Contest.® She's an expressive performance artist, mask maker, model, facilitator and writer. She's passionate about communicating the human experience through expressive art, movement, dance, video and writing. Pash is author of *Love Song to Sedona*, has a Masters in Communication and has received numerous arts-related grants. She's 47 and has lived in Sedona on and off for thirty-four years. [www.unmaskit.com]

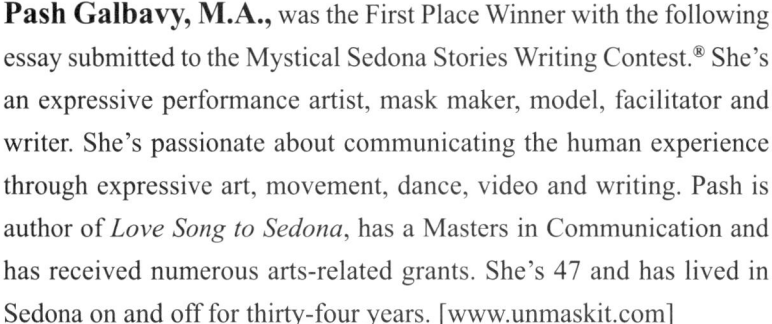

"Ever heard of the Hillside Strangler?"

It seemed an odd question to ask a hitchhiking girl. He picked me up and we drove several miles together in silence up Pacific Coast Highway, past County Line, along the beach, and now he wanted to know what? Weird!

The curly-haired driver with dark sunglasses stared rigidly at the road ahead. His body seemed constrained somehow, like his skin was too tight.

"Of course I've heard of him," I said, and brushed a wayward strand of blonde hair from my face. It was in all the papers. Someone was kidnapping young women and girls, sometimes raping and torturing them, and leaving their naked bodies on hillsides around Los Angeles.

"What would you do if he picked you up?" A slight grin tugged at the man's lips.

Santa Ana winds whipped whitecaps across the deep blue Pacific Ocean. I contemplated his question. I had a horse and was accustomed to throwing bales of hay. I also sometimes arm-wrestled grown men friends, and about half the time I would win.

"I'm pretty strong," I said. "I could probably take him on." It didn't matter that I was 13 years old. Strong was strong.

The driver suddenly made a right turn into La Jolla Canyon. His mouth curled into a strange broad smile as he hit the gas.

Get out of the car. Now! a voice in my head commanded. Everything moved in slow motion. I reached for the door handle. Opened it. Saw the blurred pavement below. Stepped out. The man grabbed my hair and held me inside as my feet and legs dragged down the road while the car continued to roll forward. A self-defense teacher recently taught that in case of an attack, scream. So I screamed. Maybe someone at the nearby campground would hear. The driver slowed, turned the car around a bend, and parked. He held my hair as he tried to get out of the passenger door while protecting his privates, which I lunged for—another self-defense trick—as I tried to escape. Once outside, under the sycamore trees with the smell of sagebrush all around, he began a head assault of well-aimed blows. I slowly fell to the ground.

A few weeks before, I'd had a peculiar dream. In it I was hiking the familiar Malibu hills near the country home my father and mother had built. My dream hike was interrupted by yet another dream, which wasn't quite like a dream at all. Suddenly, I left the hills and was free of my body. Only my consciousness seemed to shoot at high speed through a space that was surrounded by every color and no color. A disembodied voice coming from nowhere and everywhere, asked, "Do you want to go on?"

My waking life at the time was miserable. I was formerly a gifted student, but now I was partying too hard and sleeping too little. My school grades were bad. Every other week it seemed I was either running away from home or grounded. I'd recently slit my wrist, then covered it with a Band-Aid and wristwatch. I actually didn't want to go on. And yet, I also couldn't disregard nagging questions about my unknown future. What about friends I might make, loves I might have, better places I might experience if I lived long enough? And what about how devastated my mom, dad, and little sister would be if I suddenly died?

The last thought especially was unbearable. Despite all the hardships, "Yes, I want to go on," I said or maybe thought.

Suddenly, poof! I was back in my normal dream, in my normal dream body, hiking the normal dream hills.

I had chosen to live. But there in the dirt, with my arm pinned behind my back, and an insane stranger who had just beaten the crap out of me stroking my side, I wondered exactly how many more minutes or hours I had.

"Are you a virgin?" he asked.

Unsure if he wanted me to be one or not, it seemed best not to answer. I ignored him as he asked again.

Did he plan to kill me? I started to ask. "Would you please answer me a question?" I repeated this several times before he replied.

"What?"

I gulped. Maybe it was better not to know. Or maybe if I acted crazy he would leave me alone.

"Would you please answer me a question?" I repeated, over and over.

He suddenly stood up. "You really are a strong girl." Grinning broadly, he got in the car and drove away.

The ugly red blood vessel that popped in my eye during the attack was still there during the next kitchen table meeting with my very worried mom and dad. After a long discussion, we decided that it was best for me to go away for a while. Juvenile Hall was one option. Another was the co-ed boarding school in Northern Arizona that family friends had highly recommended. For once, we all agreed.

Less than two weeks after my fourteenth birthday, I sat next to my mom in the small white office of Judge Mason, the admissions officer of Verde Valley School (VVS) in Sedona, Arizona. He wore faded blue jeans and red dust-stained tennis shoes. His voice and every word were deliberate and steady. He seemed to register information, take mental notes, and observe far more than he'd let you know. Mom and I spent several hours talking with him and touring the school grounds, dorms, small classrooms, library, and spacious dining room. The adobe buildings were worn, but every room had stunning Sedona red rock views. The students and faculty were friendly.

"So, do you want to join us here?" Judge asked. His manner was easy-going, but serious.

I glanced at mom. She sat on the edge of the chair, the fingernails of her graceful hands gripped her knees. Her face looked nervous and hopeful. Judge's blue eyes smiled. I nodded hesitantly.

"You're one of the toughest-looking kids I've ever seen," he mused.

I raised my eyebrows and shrugged.

"My team has some concerns about whether you're right for this place," he continued. "But if you really want to be here, I think I can make it happen."

Judge was my champion. When my roommate tormented me into punching her, he believed that I was acting under extreme duress, which was true. When three bottles of wine were found in my room, he thought that they weren't mine, which was not true. Most importantly, he believed in me.

During the years in my new desert home, I fell in love with VVS and with Sedona. I hiked the local washes, hills, and mountains. I discovered ancient caves and Indian ruins, and I learned the names and medicinal qualities of native plants. I walked barefoot, even in the snow, because I loved the grounding, comforting feel of red earth.

I discovered a favorite spot on private property on the creek, which I regularly and quietly visited. Rumor was that a caretaker with a shotgun watched over the place, but I never saw a soul. At this special spot, defensiveness relaxed as I baked naked on rocks and swam in the waters. Restlessness calmed as I stood beneath the wind whispering through cottonwood trees, and breathed in the scents of pine and juniper. The difference between behaving wildly, and living in harmony with the wilds gradually became clear.

As graduation neared, one evening I sat on the small hill behind the school, called Cow Pie—a massively wide flattened red rock. Two ravens clacked overhead as the setting sun ignited gold fire across Cathedral and Seven Warriors—the school's mountainous northern sentinels. I contemplated the past and future as I observed VVS below with its white buildings and red roofs. I marveled at the wonder of knowing every person who lived there and having so many friends. I recalled the peculiar dream that presaged my hitchhiking attack, and was grateful that in the dream I had chosen to live. The feeling I had then was right. Life did change for the better and I was grateful to survive to enjoy it.

I faced the sun setting above Mingus Mountain and marveled at the reds, yellows, and purples erupting across the horizon. As the sunlight faded, a lone glow appeared above the dark cottonwoods lining the creek in the distance. I didn't know what that light came from, but it turned on faithfully every night. I'd seen it there since first watching sunsets from Cow Pie four years earlier. The light marked the special, private place on the creek where I still went whenever I had time. I wondered where I would go once I graduated, and how I would ever get back to this land I loved.

Three months later, I was back at my parent's house in California and working part time on an organic farm in the hills. There I met 25 year-old Marty Landa, another nature aficionado and desert lover. His mane of dark wavy hair and his karate-cut biceps made me swoon.

Together we traveled the US and the world. We saw many stunning places and even lived a number of years in Australia, where we received undergraduate literature and media production degrees. But nowhere provided the sense of place I'd felt in Sedona. I dreamed weekly of returning to that high desert home.

Marty and I eventually attended graduate school in Nevada. Because we preferred privacy from neighbors, we rented a large house trailer on a couple of sparse acres in a small town outside of Las Vegas. Life was full and stressful. We commuted to the University, and we worked full-time to develop a multimedia production for Paramount Parks at the Las Vegas Hilton.

One day I received a large letter in the mail from VVS. It contained an 8.5"x11" catalog with a cover picture of Cathedral and Seven Warriors—the view from Cow Pie. I pinned the photo to my workroom wall to remind me of the red rocks and what it was like to feel bliss and magic, sensations that seemed all but forgotten. Also in the VVS envelope was a letter stating that after many years away from the school, Judge Mason had returned and was its admissions counselor once again. He was to be in Las Vegas to visit with potential students! I called and invited him to dinner. He invited us to visit the school for possible work.

With the Paramount project finished and our Master's thesis nearly complete, Marty and I arrived in Sedona with plans to find work and a home. Someone told us that the White House Inn was the first, last, and only brothel in Sedona. Whether or not that was true, we found the cheapest rooms in town there. The receptionist was a silver-haired man with a Mona Lisa smile and stoned-looking eyes.

"Do you happen to know of any houses on a piece of land that might be for rent?" Marty inquired. We'd been asking everyone we met.

An incense stick wafted patchouli from the clerk's desk. He hummed Stravinsky's 9th off key and kept time with his left pinkie as he filled out the form for our week's stay. When there was an interval in his musical opus, he gazed past us to admire something remarkable on the empty wall at our backs. He smiled into the air, paused a dramatic half-beat, then said, "Home is where the soul lives. Know your soul and you're home."

Marty and I glanced at each other with raised eyebrows.

The man pushed the form toward Marty to sign. He theatrically pulled a room key from a row of keys on the wall and handed them to Marty in a motion just short of a two-step.

"Top of the stairs turn left and you're there." We thanked him and hurriedly started to leave. "Put an ad in the Personals section of the paper," he added. "Everyone reads the personals."

Halfway out the door, we paused.

"A personals ad in the paper to find where we want to live?" I asked.

The man pulled back his shoulders, cleared his throat, and stood taller as if to begin a speech. "I graduated with two PhDs from Yale, but I didn't learn what I know there. You have to manifest what you want." He smiled broadly and nodded all around as if to imaginary cheering. I half expected him to take a bow. Instead, he was suddenly sitting back at his desk humming and filling out paperwork.

A few days later our ad appeared in the *Red Rock News*:

```
Ideal tenants seeking dream private
quiet rental on acreage property.
Non-smokers. No pets. No children.
```

Two months later, we were renting a studio in back of a house off Upper Red Rock Loop Road. The landlord's two children banged on the walls at night and shouted all day in the yard. There was a flood of responses to our ad. We'd heard about enough private, quiet apartment duplexes, and seen enough dream-homes-in-a-neat-neighborhood-row to lose hope of ever finding a place to call home in Sedona. The potential job and living situation at VVS had not come through, and our intentions to attend Prescott College for grad work hadn't worked out either. We finally pulled our ridiculous and expensive ad, and pondered daily why we ever thought to try to live in such a small and expensive town.

"Hey!" Marty shouted, as he bolted upright in bed and woke me from a deep slumber. "I just dreamed about the place we're going to move into!"

"Huh?" I rubbed my eyes and tried to focus on the digital clock on the bedside table—3:07 a.m.

"It's in Sedona. It's over a hundred acres and has sort of a barn with a hitching post. It was a lucid dream. It's our new place!"

I sighed and rolled away. "Wonderful," I grumbled. "Go back to sleep."

A couple of weeks later, we sat at the small kitchen table eating breakfast and contemplating our next move—maybe California or Australia? The smell of the oatmeal I burned permeated the small space. The landlord's children played irksome screaming games outside. Marty tallied our finances on scrap paper and shook his head. We had heard the joke that to make a fortune in Sedona you had to bring two fortunes. It seemed true. What little we had was going fast.

The phone rang.

"Are you the ideal tenants?" a man inquired.

"Yes," I sighed, "but we're having a heck of a time finding the dream rental."

"We've got that," he said. "It's just a small house, but you might like it. It's near the creek."

As he described the location, I got goose bumps.

"I think I know that place—"

Hy and Hellie Blythe had a subscription to the *Red Rock News*, which was delivered to them twice weekly at their ranch in California.

They'd been seeing our ad there. We had to wait two weeks before they would be in Sedona to meet them.

At last, Marty and I drove over the cattle guard and under the large, faded, hand-painted sign that read 'Hi Lo Ranch.' We passed a huge metal airplane hangar with an old tractor and ancient farm equipment around it. As we headed down a long dirt road I could barely contain my excitement.

"I'm sure this is the property I used to sneak onto when I was a kid!" I said. We drove past giant old cottonwood trees, a pasture, and a creek-water irrigation ditch. We hadn't even arrived and already I felt I was home.

We parked in front of a modest, single-story, white adobe ranch house surrounded by a small well-manicured lawn. Opposite was an old wooden shed and six-car carport attached to a wooden corral. Adjacent was a two-story barn.

"Well, hello!" A screen door banged behind the tall, handsome older man who strode from the house. He wore a white cowboy hat, a pressed white shirt with jeans and cowboy boots. He heartily shook our hands. A slight, smiling, slender, white-haired woman with a hand-embroidered shirt and skirt followed.

"Greetings!" Her eyes sparkled with child-like joy.

Hy and Hellie took us through 'Lo house,' the house that they stayed in when they visited. Just up the driveway they showed us 'Mid house,' a 2-bedroom, 1000-square-foot old red rock house.

"This would be yours," Hy said. The view from the bedroom, porch, and backyard was Cathedral and Seven Warriors, just like on the VVS brochure cover!

Further up the road we walked past the third old red rock structure, Hi house, where tenants lived who ran cows and farmed some of the property.

We stood on a bluff and looked out across the expanse of Hi-Lo

Ranch and beyond. A cool autumn breeze teased our hair. A raven swooshed overhead. Oak Creek meandered amidst orange-leafed sycamores below. Across the creek was a field of garlic and a dozen-plus grazing deer. To the far north stood Thunder Mountain. Cathedral rose in the northeast next to Seven Warriors. Further east was the red roofs of VVS. And to the west, Mingus Mountain. Hy pointed to various landmarks marking the boundaries of the pristine, 115 acre property. We stared in awe.

"We call this the jewel in the king's crown," Hy chuckled. His voice carried the soft pride of love.

Thirty years before, the Blythe's traded a castle with 26 miles of Scottish coastline to Stan Avery (of Avery label fame) for Hi-Lo Ranch. But since then, between grandchildren and their other California ranch, Hy and Hellie only infrequently traveled to Sedona. Because their last caretaker died, they needed someone new to watch over the place.

"So, do you think you could live here?" Hy tipped back his hat to look us in the eyes.

Dumbfounded, Marty and I nodded affirmatively.

"Could you manage $350 a month?"

Incredulous, we vehemently nodded favorably again.

"But we don't want tenants. We want friends."

Marty coughed. "Uh, I think we could be friends!"

Yes!" I finally found my voice.

Hellie clapped her hands and giggled. "I knew it. I had a feeling."

"Three people fell through for the position," Hy said. In all the years they had the ranch, they always found someone they knew or who was referred to them. "But Hellie and her intuition. She kept seeing that ad!"

Sixteen-and-a-half years after I had first left Sedona, we moved in as caretakers for Hi-Lo Ranch. The first evening, as we carried boxes from our car, I paused along the stone path in the front yard. An old dead saguaro cactus trunk leaned decoratively against the house. For some reason its shape made me think of the hitching post from Marty's dream.

"Hey, remember that dream about the hundred acres and the hitching post?" We dropped our boxes in the grass and walked in the fading light down the driveway to the barn. In front of it stood a sturdy old wooden hitching post.

Marty's eyes misted. "Yes, this is what I saw," he said softly.

We hugged. Crickets chirped above the sound of the creek rushing in the distance. A breeze cooled my face and rattled the yellow cottonwood leaves hanging above the water ditch. Gazing over Marty's shoulder, I gasped.

Beyond the silhouette of a giant dead sycamore was a full moon rising above Seven Warriors. We stared—awestruck. An owl hooted. A chorus of coyotes yipped.

Slowly, we turned back toward the house. Next to the shed, a light automatically switched on and began glowing softly from the top of the ancient gas pump. I gasped again.

"I used to see that light when I was a kid at VVS! I could see it from Cow Pie." My eyes teared.

Marty squeezed my hand. "We're home."

We found our rhythm with the seasons at Hi-Lo. Fall was when the leaves were raked. We trapped and relocated skunks and raccoons that tore up the lawns in their autumn search for grubs. Wood was chopped to prepare for the quiet winter cold and snow. In spring, trees and bushes overgrowing rooftops and paths were trimmed. Sprinklers were repaired, and the water ditch cleared. Summer was for mowing, weed whacking and watering. Also sunbathing and creek floats. Sunset watching from the hill facing Mingus Mountain was essential year round. And whenever we heard trespassers, as often as Marty bolted to chase them away, I wished they knew just to be quiet!

The history of the land became our history. On the hillside were ancient Indian pottery shards. In the garlic field was the original 1800s Sedona schoolhouse fireplace and chimney. A homesteader's old campsite hid against a red embankment. Sour descendants of copper miner's wine grapes grew by the swimming hole. And Hy told stories about senators and statesmen who passed through.

Our clan expanded to include the muskrats and beaver that built homes on the water's edge, the catfish that spawned in the shallow cattails, and the red and blue dragonflies that mated on creek rocks. Our next of kin became the deer standing on hind legs to eat plums from the Lo house tree, bald eagles nesting in the sycamore tops, and roaming javelina families.

At least twice yearly, I returned to Malibu to visit family. One summer evening in 1998, nearly twenty years after first moving to Sedona, my mom, sister, and I sat in my old bedroom and settled on the couch to watch a TV show about the Hillside Strangler. My sister was a crime buff, and of course, we all remembered the publicity surrounding the infamous Los Angeles case. When a photo of Kenneth Bianchi, one of the two murderous cousins appeared, adrenaline suddenly rushed through my body and my heartbeat skyrocketed.

"That's the guy! The one who beat me up hitchhiking!"

We watched details of the story, and my brush with that strange piece of history took on new meaning. Of the twelve known girls and women murdered by Bianchi and his cousin Angelo Buono, ten were killed in the four months surrounding my hitchhiking encounter. Yet somehow, one hardened, strong and lucky teenager escaped.

Back home on the ranch a couple months later, I sat in a summer dress and swung on the faded wooden love seat in our back yard. My toes grazed the top of damp and freshly mowed bluegrass. A mourning dove coo-coo'd in the field beyond the weather-worn back fence. A Jacobs Ladder of sunlight lit Cathedral's red pillars against a steel-gray backdrop of storm clouds. I breathed the heavenly scent of wet earth delivered through an earlier rain shower.

A gust of wind threatened another downpour as I scanned *Kudos* weekly newspaper offerings. Tautly holding the paper's pages, I perused a story about a local keyboard artist, Bob Grogan, who was to play that weekend at Canyon Moon Theater. Suddenly, I caught my breath. Earlier in his life, Grogan was the primary detective in breaking the Hillside Strangler case! Clutching the paper as raindrops spattered, I ran into our old red rock house. I grabbed the phone book from the top of the refrigerator, sat on the living room couch with the phone beside me, and looked up 'Grogan.'

As Bob and I spoke, I thanked him for his previous work. Life had come full circle.

POSTSCRIPT: Every sweet season must pass, and eventually the ranch sold. Seven years after starting, our caretaking gig ended. And now, although we no longer live on that ideal property, Marty and I are still in Sedona, and we're proof that dreams come true here.

CHAPTER SEVEN
A Spirit Quest

Robin Lee Strom, PT has been a physical therapist since 1977 and has continued in practice in Sedona since 1992 with a Body-Mind-Spirit emphasis. She's extensively trained in integrated manual therapy, but her focus is on the holistic side and what is presenting within her patient in the moment. Robin is 57 and a resident of Sedona for three years (1992-1995).

In the 1980s I was living in San Francisco and had a group of friends who used to discuss spiritual books. One interesting thing we did together was art therapy to access the subconscious. We also all went to Jungian therapy (individually of course). The principle behind Jungian therapy is to look at subconscious patterns. By 1985, I was going to Jungian therapy once a week and continued for three more years. I began opening myself up as I explored my dreams and subconscious processes.

In one of my dreams I met an Indian woman who was calling me to go on retreat. Coincidentally, during this time my friend Jan told me about a woman who gave retreats in Sedona, and that during an upcoming stay in Santa Rosa, California, she'd be giving individualized sessions. When she told me that, I was immediately struck with a 'knowing' that I wasn't only going to meet with her in Santa Rosa, I was going to go to Sedona on retreat with this very woman. After I shared this awareness with Jan, she was incredulous. She told me I would have to talk to this woman first and set up an appointment with her before I'd be allowed to go on retreat with her.

When this woman visited Santa Rosa, I set up the appointment and upon arrival, a short, dark, stocky yet lean Native American man was there with a book of pictures from their tribe. He had on a tan hat with an owl feather protruding forward from the left rim. As I glanced at the photo album, there was one photo of the very woman who had appeared to me in my dream! I was stunned by the confirmation of the dream. By the same token, I knew this was the shaman I was destined to meet. Embarrassed to even confess such a preposterous thing to this stranger holding the photo album, I pointed to the photo of the woman and asked, "Who's this?"

"She's the person you're going to meet today for your appointment," he said.

Suddenly, a door opened and a matronly, buxom, short Native American woman appeared, her hair jet black with shades of purple loosely held back by a barrette. She was wearing a white high-waisted embroidered smock.

She motioned for me to come in, introduced herself, and asked, "What brings you here today?"

I was quite nervous about being perceived by her in some strange way. However, the words kind of fell off my lips as I explained quite openly and honestly, "I met you in a dream."

She smiled and asked with no surprise on her face, "How can I help you?"

"I'm on a spiritual quest and I'd like to be assisted in this journey."

The session lasted one hour. I have little memory of what transpired during this time because I was literally in an altered state in her presence. At the end, I clearly recall saying to her, "Thank you. I'll see you at the retreat."

She didn't react in any way to acknowledge that I would even be at her retreat. I turned and walked to the sofa in the other room, sat down and waited for my friend to pick me up as the shaman went into her room with the next person. About fifteen minutes later, the door opened and the same Native American woman leaned out and said to me, "I'll see you at the retreat."

Minutes later my ride came.

While still living in San Francisco, I went to the shaman's workshops for a week in Sedona twice a year to learn about releasing my conditioning, habits, immature emotions and thoughts in an experiential way. We did releasing, purification, rebirthing, and naming ceremonies during many of the workshops.

In one particular workshop, we did a rosemary bath to purify ourselves to release any blocks to spirit before undertaking this quest. We set up camp in Boynton Canyon, and then around midnight, we were taken by truck probably a couple miles toward Devil's Bridge to an area about two and a half miles down the road from where our campsite was set up. On this quest, we were to walk ten feet apart from each other. The purpose of the Spirit Walk was that each person was to be connected internally—to the immanent Spirit that resides in each of us—with full awareness and presence to the energy of this Spirit. Among twelve of us, my position in the line was second to the last with a man named Michael following behind me. As we slowly walked, I quieted my energy and fully connected to the Earth and opened up my heart to the Heavens. Although we were in the woods and it was a gorgeous night, my focus was not with the stars or the clouds, but rather internally. There was a stark stillness and lightness within me and all around me. All the cells in my body felt an effervescence.

I was unaware of Michael's presence directly behind me until no more than five minutes into the Walk I realized Michael and I were in a distinctly different physical dimension. I had never experienced anything like this before. A reality shift had occurred. Immediately, I could see hundreds of glowing colored light spheres no more than half an inch in diameter. They were clung to trees, shrubs, and on the ground—everywhere! These self-illuminating spheres were pure energy in the midst of the high desert landscape. I stopped and turned to Michael who also had stopped walking. He was as awestruck as me.

"Oh my God!" he uttered.

As Michael and I stood by a tree, the dots of energy were all around. I was in a state of absolute wonderment. We both extended our index finger, each of us touching a different light sphere. The one I touched was pure white. Michael touched an all-red sphere. The spheres ran the color range of a rainbow, but each sphere held only one color. I felt an electrical-like force at my fingertip upon connection to this energy. Michael said he felt the same thing.

We suddenly became aware of the others on the Spirit Walk, and although we looked ahead, we could not see our companions anywhere. We could hear sounds of their voices, but it was like hearing voices underwater. We were unable to understand what they were saying. We realized we were invisible to them and they were invisible to us. Michael confirmed the same experience.

We continued the Spirit Walk with lightness in our energy body. I was in a different physical/space dimension in my same physical body. As we approached the campsite, we arrived and saw all the people anxiously looking at us, questioning us about where we had been for so long!

The Shaman must have known that we were in a different space. She looked at Michael and me, then addressed the whole group. "Come—gather around the campfire now so we can speak about our experiences."

We were all steered toward the campfire with instructions to individually share our experiences on the Spirit Walk. A couple others talked about how they saw bats flying and that two people had started screaming and dodging to get away from the bats. This was the noise that Michael and I became alerted to when we heard 'the underwater voices' and realized that the others were not in the same space that we were.

I would never have shared my experiences had it not been for Michael who had taken the identical journey. I shared that my experience was that of being in another physical dimension right here in the same physical location as the others, but that I had somehow accessed a portal to this other dimension.

It was the Shaman who originally brought me to Sedona, but it was one prophetic dream in November of 1989 that stands out as unique. In that dream I recognized that I would get married to my boyfriend, but then I'd be moving to Sedona without him to do my work, and that this would happen within two years. In November, two years to the month of that dream, I moved to Sedona and separated from my husband to do my work as a physical therapist in body, mind, spirit and consciousness healing. When I was driving from California with my U-Haul of possessions, as I crossed the border from California to Arizona, I knew I was coming home.

POSTSCRIPT: On August 4, 2012, after this story was accepted for publication in this book, I was watching the BBC American debut of *The Science of Doctor Who*. This is a science fiction TV program that's been around since 1963 exploring time travel, wormholes, parallel universes and dimensions, cyborgs, and so forth. Michio Kaku, Ph.D., one of my favorite people and a theoretical physicist, explained the possibility that our world is like an expanding soap bubble and that it's possible another 'soap bubble expanding universe' can be attached to ours by a gateway or portal connection. I know this is possible. That seemed to perfectly describe my experience!

Part III

Dreams and Visions

"In sleep, fantasy takes the form of dreams. But in waking life too, we continue to dream beneath the threshold of consciousness . . ."
Carl Jung, MD, In *Problems of Modern Psychotherapy* (1929)

Two of the most distinguished minds in psychoanalysis in the 20th century —Carl Jung and Sigmund Freud—could not agree on the simplest purpose of dreams. Therefore, to attempt to define *a vision* within the limitations of science would seem to prove its very impossibility, save for those who experience it.

CHAPTER EIGHT
Field of a Dream

John A. Tamiazzo, Ph.D., is an expert in the fields of human potential, neuroscience and transpersonal psychology. He's authored two books: *Returning to the Land of Oz* (Eloquent Books, 2010) and *Love and be Loved* (Borgo Press, 1986). John is 64 and has lived in Sedona one year. [www.landofozworkshops.blogspot.com]

On September 6, 2011 in the little town of Cambria, along the coast of California north of San Luis Obispo, I had an amazing dream. I was invited to play baseball as a guest player for a major league baseball team. Over 9 innings I hit 4 home runs and became an instant celebrity. I had never had a dream with such clarity, depth and realism. When I awoke, I wrote the dream down in my journal and spent the next few months trying to figure out what this powerful dream was trying to tell me.

I played with the imagery and symbolism of 9 players and 4 home runs. I was most intrigued by the symbolism of the 4 home runs, so I put my time and focus there. I did some research and found out that only fifteen times in major league baseball history had a player hit 4 home runs in a single game. Bobby Lowe of the Boston Beaneaters first achieved this in 1894. Lou Gehrig of the New York Yankees did it in 1932. Gil Hodges of the Brooklyn Dodgers did it in 1950. Willie Mays of the San Francisco Giants did it in 1961. What was equally amazing was that my dream was telling me that I was the 16th to accomplish this great feat. If you think about how many players have played the game in the last hundred years, how many innings these players have played, how many balls have been pitched to them, that only 15 elite superstars hit 4 home runs (prior to me achieving it in my dream) is truly an extraordinary statistic.

Prophetic dreams are more commonplace than one might think. Our unconscious mind is always trying to bring its wisdom to our attention through synchronicities, books we happen to pick up to read, people we meet who say something life changing, and dreams that come to us during the night. Dreams are one of the most important ways the unconscious communicates with us. What, I asked, was my unconscious trying to tell me through my intriguing and inspiring dream?

Every time I read the dream and played with the imagery, I wondered what the 4 home runs would look like for me in the coming weeks and months. What form would they take? Would the dream unfold in my current home state of California? Would I have to move and change location for these symbolic home runs to manifest? I was approaching the interpretation of this dream, therefore, as a prophetic dream that would hopefully come true in some spectacular fashion. While I had remarkable dreams in the past, no dreams were quite like this one. I felt a huge change was right around the corner. Sometimes you can just feel it. I was going to be invited to play in an arena I never played in before and score big time!

In discussing the dream with my girlfriend, we decided that the dream would most likely manifest someplace else. We had discussed moving many times before and Northern California was at the top of our list. The important thing was to find a fantastic job in a fabulous place.

I began a job search in the San Francisco Bay Area. For over a month I looked at job sites like craigslist and americanjobs.com, but one day I did something different. Out of the blue I clicked on 'location' to see what was going on in the job market across the country. As the states popped up alphabetically, my eyes glanced atop the list. The first state I saw was Alabama—no interest in moving to the deep south; Alaska—no interest in moving to a very cold climate so far away; Arizona—a good prospect and right next door; and lastly, Arkansas—no interest in living there either. I clicked on Arizona and the first job to appear was for The Sedona Community Center.

Arizona and especially Sedona intrigued me because I had a

reference point having first been to Sedona in early December, 1992. I remembered it well. I was attending a four-day Milton Erickson Hypnosis Conference in Phoenix and decided to drive up to Sedona afterward. What sparked my interest in going there was the enthusiasm that someone shared at the conference in reference to Sedona. Her excitement made an impression on me. The hotel where I was staying had a directory for the Sedona area and as I scanned the hotel listings, *L'Auberge de Sedona* grabbed my attention. I gave them a call and booked my stay for three nights at $100 a night. It turned out to be a charming hotel in a spellbinding setting. I remember taking hikes to mesmerizing vortexes and being surrounded by the awesome beauty of the red rocks.

The Sedona Community Center was searching for an Executive Director. I scanned through the job responsibilities and professional requirements and knew immediately that I had the background and skills that would qualify me. I emailed my application. Within a few weeks a Skype interview was set up. Following this was an in-person interview in Sedona on the 6th of January, 2012.

After that interview I was asked to go back to my hotel room and they would call with a decision within the hour. At 2:30 p.m. on the 6th of January, I was offered the job. Delighted beyond words that I was offered a fantastic job in a fabulous place, I went back to my hotel room and called a property management company about a home for lease in West Sedona that was advertised in the *Red Rock News*. I made an appointment to see it at 3:30 p.m. When I walked into the living room of this beautiful home I was awestruck by the views of Thunder Mountain, Coffee Pot, Cathedral Rock, and other spectacular red rock formations in the distance. I grabbed it on the spot. So, within an hour I had a fantastic job, in an amazing place, and a gorgeous home. Three home runs! What would be the 4th home run, I mused?

Once I got back home to California I called three moving

companies to schedule a move to Sedona by the end of January. Either the dates didn't work or the bids were too high. I got a tip from one of the Sedona Community Center Board members to try Sedona Moving Company. I called them and coincidentally they were going to be in California in two weeks moving a couple from Sedona to a town about three hours away from where I was living. Instead of driving back to Sedona with an empty moving truck, they would come by and pick up my stuff and give me a great price. Also, they agreed to keep my things in storage at no additional cost until I arrived two weeks later.

Four home runs: An amazing place, a fantastic job, a gorgeous home with mesmerizing views, and a move that was divinely orchestrated. After I got hired I discovered that, just like in my dream, there are two teams at The Center each with 9 players: 9 board members serving on the Board of Directors and, including me, 9 staff members. It is my job responsibility to inspire these two teams to work harmoniously and enjoyably together; to smile and play as we serve the residents of the greater Sedona community.

I may never be inducted into the baseball hall of fame, but I'm the proudest guy in town with the deepest satisfaction and joy in knowing that the Sedona Community Center delivers meals to those who cannot provide them for themselves, provides low cost meals to the community at The Center during lunch time, and offers fantastic brain enhancement programs and critical services to the greater Sedona community. The team I play on improves quality of life for people every day.

The second week on the job, I attended a luncheon sponsored by a local organization, *Keep Sedona Beautiful,* honoring the Sedona Community Center as a Sedona Treasure. What a great way to begin a new job, knowing I work for an organization so highly regarded and treasured in the community. I am delighted that I'm here doing what I do on this 'baseball field' called Sedona!

POSTSCRIPT: On May 8, 2012, Josh Hamilton of the Texas Rangers hit four home runs in one game. The article mentioned that he's the 16th player in baseball history to accomplish this great feat. In Eastern Tradition a question is often raised, is this so-called reality we live in really a dream and are our nightly dreams reality? I know the truth. He's the 17th player. I hit my home runs in January!

CHAPTER NINE
The Birthday Party

Miki Butterworth and husband Bob are retired from Houston, and care for rental properties. Miki worked as a singer/guitarist for twenty-six years and spent fifteen years owning a women's boutique and world artifact store. She dabbles in several art mediums, performance art, writing and acting. Miki is 66 and has lived in Sedona for ten years.

I was notified in late August that the movie theater adjacent to my boutique in Houston was to be torn down and that the fenced-off area surrounding the demolition would necessitate my store closing for a month. After a day of indignation I re-centered myself and realized this might be a gift and just what I needed—time away.

After eighteen years of dealing with the public I was losing the love I always had for my business and was on a fast track to burnout. As I contemplated what I might do with this time, my desire to travel through the Southwest came to mind. I had been fortunate to travel to many countries for my business, but hopping a plane for five days and back was different from touring a vast area. This can only be done by car and weeks of leisure time.

Honoring the nudging of my psyche and my curiosity about a prophetic dream I recently had about a life change coming, I talked with Bob about taking off on an adventure.

Three days later, Bob—already retired—and I left the big city of Houston for the open road. Camping gear, road maps and high spirits in tow we made our way westward, our voices harmonizing *Route 66.*

Fifteen hundred miles and three weeks later having explored Mesa Verde, Chaco Canyon, Monument Valley, Moab, Canyon de Chelly and the Grand Canyon, we reached our turnaround point—Las Vegas. After two days in the adult playground and travel-weary, we decided to cut short the tourist attractions, and planned for the return trip to Texas.

Before leaving Houston we had been implored by several friends to spend a few days in the town of Sedona that lies between Flagstaff and Phoenix. Reaching Flagstaff our map showed a canyon road circumventing the interstate, passing through Sedona and reconnecting. We'd be able to tell people, "Yes, we went to Sedona," and yet cruise through and make Phoenix for the night.

Five miles into the canyon, I was awe-stricken. A thousand feet below the overlooks was a sea of towering pines. Bob maneuvered hair-pin turns and as if at a tennis match, our eyes darted from one breathtaking vision to another. Windows and sunroof open, the crisp September air was invigorating and the sounds of the rushing creek that followed the narrow blacktop delighted my senses. Monstrous roots of the sycamore hugged the water's edge and our silence gave way to gasps and deep breaths as if inhaled deeply enough we could carry all this back with us. Twenty miles of this travel-treat and a descent of twenty-five hundred feet, cacti started to dot the landscape.

Emerging from the canyon and rounding a curve, an entirely different world unfolded. Giant red rocks jutting hundreds of feet high rose straight up out of the earth in a landscape reminiscent of some forgotten prehistoric era. I expected to see a dinosaur cross our path at any moment.

My voice breaking, I asked, "Bob . . . are you thinking?—"

"Yes!" he finished my thought.

We wound around, through and in between this ethereal beauty as the late afternoon sun shining on the stone towers turned them into glowing, iridescent works of art. A total sense of well-being coursed through our veins. Bob pulled into the parking area of the first business we saw. We got out and asked the sales person standing in the doorway where we could find a real estate agent.

It was easy to understand Sedona's reputation as a spiritual hub.

Just the imposing size and colors of the buttes, as we learned they were called, made one feel small and want to surrender control to a higher power. I'm certain most everyone coming through Sedona is awed, but there was more here for both Bob and me. I'm a spontaneous person, but not so Bob. He doesn't like change or surprises, which is why when I had the dream a few months earlier about the coming of a change in our life, I gave him forewarning. He had learned over our time together that when I had a certain kind of dream, one could count on it coming to fruition.

It did not strike either of us as strange that we were spending the afternoon and early evening seriously looking at homes on this first day. We got a motel for the night and settled into dinner at a small Thai restaurant.

We called several friends that evening to tell them we were moving and of course they didn't believe us. After a few days we returned to Houston to put the wheels in motion. Having a business to shut down and four rental houses, we knew there was much to do. We researched Sedona homes online and kept revisiting one in particular.

The following month we returned to Sedona with an appointment to see ten houses. We arrived the evening before our appointment and decided to get a map and find the house we were so charmed by on the Internet. As we pulled up the hill on Courthouse Butte, sitting right at the base of an 850-foot butte, there it was! A tear ran down my cheek. Joy, humility, gratitude and a childlike wonder overcame me. *I knew I was home.* I looked over at Bob. Puddles had formed in his lower lids. We circled the block five times. Our next door neighbor later recalled to us she remarked to her husband that day, "There goes that little red car again."

We returned to the motel and called the agent. We asked if she could change the schedule so we could see Courthouse Butte first the following morning.

"What if this is the right place?" Bob asked. We realized we would need three months, at least, to make things work. We sure couldn't pay for two houses.

The next morning I entered the home carrying a video camera. As I went from room to room, I spoke into the camera, "This is our entrance hall," and opening a door, "this is our guest bathroom, and . . ."

As we continued through the house we couldn't believe that everything on our needs and wish list was there. Things that were unclear from the Internet pictures were now crystal clear, such as the unrestricted corner lot, large windows that overlooked the red rocks, and a beautiful desert scape, a workshop in the garage for Bob, an open floor plan and arched niches for my artifacts. Everything was there!

We made an offer on the spot and within two hours it was accepted. We learned that the owners had made a pact that if their home didn't sell by the date on which we made the offer, they would pull it off the market and remain in Sedona. The agent stated that the couple had one other request to be put in the contract, that they be able to lease it back from us for three months. They needed more time to vacate. We high-fived one another and laughed.

Back in Houston I had one employee I was concerned about leaving without a job. She said, coincidently, she had just been given a wonderful opportunity and was thrilled she could take it without leaving me in a bind.

My number one supplier was a major concern for me. How might my business closing affect her business? Over the years we had become dependent on one another. I was her biggest wholesale client and she was my main supplier. I called her the day I returned and asked her to lunch. She said she was just going to call me. She had something she needed to discuss with me. Over a tasty lunch we laughed (almost hysterically) as she related that she and her husband had decided to retire and close their business. We created a joint going out-of-business sale that worked out wonderfully. It also just happened that my six-year commercial lease would be up in three months. It couldn't have been orchestrated any smoother. All plans, agendas and perceived obstacles continued to resolve in an uncanny way, both for time and money.

Three months later we pulled into the driveway of our new Sedona home, red car, U-Haul and second truck in tandem. Within five minutes the neighbors were greeting us with well wishes, genuine smiles and offers of help. In the second week we were given a *Welcome to the neighborhood and get acquainted* party! Within two months we were an integral part of the whole.

If you don't feel the synchronicity yet, let me tell you of my birthday four months later. It was not yet known that I had come through years of flashbacks, regressions and efforts to heal trauma from childhood abuse. Birthdays were usually painful. I was living on an isolated farm with my grandma. One birthday the mailman drove out with a package. Grandma said I was being too silly over a package so it would be put up on top of the fridge until I could reclaim my dignity. Three days later she allowed me to open it. Making sure not to show a trace of excitement, I folded back the tissue revealing a walking doll. She grabbed it from its box, played with it for a few minutes and then declared, "We'll just put this away 'til your older!" But older would never come.

On my 9th birthday, Mama, whom I had not seen or heard from in six months, made an unexpected trip to grandma's farm. She scrubbed me thoroughly and covered me in all white—dress, slip, socks, shoes and flowered headband—a pristine fantasy in white. "Pure as the new fallen snow, just like my little darling," Mama said.

She drove me thirty miles to a strange house with nine strange children to produce a Kodak moment and a story for the Sunday edition of the *Tulsa World*. This was one of her many attempts to reassure herself of my purity and remain in denial of the rape I had suffered at age four when she had left me all alone at home.

I had told Bob that Sedona would be a new start for me where my past would not define me. The neighbor backing to us, upon hearing it was to be my birthday, invited us all over for cake that special day. She said the idea of a big child's party 'just came to her' so she put the wheels in motion.

When I arrived, a cardboard glittered tiara was placed on my head. Among the balloons and crepe paper streamers we played pin the tail on the donkey, blew bubbles and drenched each other in water gun fights. Long past my prime, immersed in childhood antics I missed so long ago, with a lump in my throat and joy in my heart, I blew out all my candles.

CHAPTER TEN
The Mindful Teacher

Richard E. Carmen, Au.D., holds a Doctor of Audiology degree from the Arizona School of Health Sciences (a division of the Kirksville College of Osteopathic Medicine). He's a nationally recognized author and well-published scientist who's written extensively in the healthcare field as a regular contributor for many peer-reviewed journals and healthcare industry publications. Richard is 67 years old and has been a Sedona resident for twenty-four years.

When I was in audiology research and clinical practice in Los Angeles in the 1970s, I was also on a very private path exploring the mysteries of the human potential. I read with much interest a variety of books on body, mind and spirit; the nature of death and afterlife; potentials of space travel and probabilities of extraterrestrial life; prayer; meditation; extrasensory perception (ESP); the credibility of mediumship; the lives of highly regarded intuits like Edgar Casey and Nostradamus; and I did comparative research on bibles 100 years and older and discovered line-for-line opposite scripture within the same religious sects.

As it turned out, I was ripe for the picking by 1985 when I met Adele Tinning—a transmedium living in San Diego who had mastered the mid-1800s art of table-tipping. Adele ultimately strengthened my budding Buddhist conviction that *all things are possible* since she did the impossible.

One day I went for a session with Adele. She sat down on her wooden chair at the kitchen table and rested her plump, rotund body comfortably. She looked so much older than her 77 years—her soft face, rosy cheeks and neck all seasoned with deep grooves and wrinkles. She pulled aside a tuff of short curly white hair which sprang right back over her forehead, then stared into my eyes as I sat opposite her. After a minute or two of settling into the moment, she took a deep breath and released it.

"Okay honey," she said, breathing heavily, teasing me into the session with her warm, broad smile and charm, "let's be certain the spirit from the other side you wish to bring in is the spirit it claims to be. So in your mind, ask this person a very specific question. Don't tell me who it is. Don't say anything. Just *think* about the person in your mind."

I came to this session already knowing it was my brilliant friend, Gene, who had died years earlier. In my mind I thought attentively about him. At age eighteen he had been hired as an inventor at General Electric. However, he struggled emotionally and financially most of his life. I did what I could when I could to help him—to little avail. He was on heavy psychotropic medications for the latter years of his life and finally passed away in rather tragic shape.

I brought back memory of a time in the 1960s when he and I realized someone had stolen all my numismatic proof sets—coins that were dated ten or fifteen years earlier. In my mind, I asked Gene, *What was it that was stolen from my house when I was a kid?*

"Okay Adele, I've asked the question in my mind."

Only a moment passed after which Adele offered one word: "coins." Despite no conversation between us, Adele was picking up on his energy as she tried to clear her glassy eyes.

"Oh my . . . he's very talented!" Adele stated. I said nothing and was very conscious not to give her any confirmation through my body language or facial expressions. I just listened. I had not told a soul who I intended to bring in during my session with her. She could not have known this was a man, let alone talented. "He's a wonderful musician and artist," she added. Gene was a classical pianist and portrait artist. As the short session progressed, she was correct on everything. What was most striking was the core truth about Gene. "He's a tortured soul, honey," she continued, "but he wants you to know that he's working on his life over there and things are actually much better."

Adele performed the same 'impossible' things time and again with thousands of people. I had seen her make errors, but the remarkable rate of consistently correct information was what was so striking. I brought many friends to see her. When she was right, she was so right to the point of names, dates, personalities, temperaments, places, specific addresses . . . there was no limit to it. She defied the laws of . . . well, *everything!* She typically confessed it was never her though. She said she was only the medium, the pathway through which this information traveled, but you knew there was so much more she wasn't telling you. She never charged a fee and sat with more than 10,000 people by the end of her 83 years. She also never charged for the thousands of books she gifted to anyone desiring to read what she wrote. Adele was modest, humble and loved every person she met.

As a witness to her abilities, as a rather objective observer and scientist, I was truly certain this was no parlor trick. While I had a few firsthand personal experiences of ESP, I presumed it to be impossible for anyone to *consistently* read thoughts. Adele's abilities didn't quite fit into my reality—albeit an ever-expanding square box. Everything on which science is based was testimony that what I witnessed was impossible. Two of the three foundations of the scientific method might hold up under scrutiny of her abilities (*observable* and *repeatable*) giving credence to her talent, but nothing was ever *measurable*. There was no way anyone seemed able to measure her abilities, although some scientists had apparently tried their hardest. Her abilities were simply a gift.

Over the next few years Adele and I became well acquainted. I and my friends would periodically leave money under her bed pillow in appreciation for her kindness because she outright refused payment. She later confided in me that NASA scientists and astronauts, in addition to many well-known Hollywood figures were regular visitors to her home and private sessions.

After reading hundreds of books, decades of searching, and ultimately meeting Adele, by 1985 I had come to the realization that we know frighteningly little about ourselves, the world and the universe. I had concluded that the world as we know it is a grand illusion. Among my many sessions with Adele, I seemed to even arrive at new insights into the nature of death itself. My former notion had been that when we die we reach some kind of nirvana or heaven, or a place of great tranquility and peace, when the other side may well merely be a progression of this side. In fact, there's more evidence to support the belief that we achieve our greatest (and fastest) life potentials and lessons on this side called *life*. This is supported by many people who have been clinically dead, only to return and report they were instructed to "Go back" or "It's not your time yet." Many who have been clinically dead even report details in the ER, right down to conversations, medical instruments and equipment used to bring them back.

Some twelve years after I had first watched the Maharishi Mahesh Yogi on television and twisted myself into a pretzel, Harvard scientist Richard Alpert, Ph.D.—aka Baba Ram Dass—(a colleague and cohort of famed Timothy Leary) published *Be Here Now* (1971). It became a pivotal book on my journey and that of millions of other hippies. 'Ram Dass' (so-named by his East Indian guru) shared marvelous insights about love, life and spirit in both his book and lectures. He was a man who essentially stepped out of science to discover his own human potential. He came to represent how anyone could attain bodhisattva—'Enlightenment' or 'Awakening'—without having to run off to India as he had done.

By December of 1984, thirteen years after reading *Be Here Now*, only the vapors of his wisdom remained in my memory. The illusions of life had arisen like alluring beasts. My unquenchable desire for female pleasure had become an illusion unto itself—misdirecting my higher purpose. It finally all came to a crescendo with Patty, who was gorgeous and sexy, sumptuous and sweet, but an alcoholic, a liar and a deceiver. I was at my wit's end. How could I have made so many poor choices in women for so many years? How could I not have recognized the landmarks that kept pulling my feathers out until I could no longer fly?

I was finally done, fed up with myself. I needed to make a change. I was ready for a shift. I blamed no one but me for the condition of my life. So New Year's Eve 1984, I spent alone at home, feeling bad that I had let Patty go, but pleased that I was willing to make this change.

I put on the soft sounds of Gregorian chants and sat mid-center on the large Chinese silk-wool rug that covered my living room floor. As I faced the fireplace on this windy evening, flames were being pulled away upward and tickled the flue. If I had learned anything in thirty-nine years, I contemplated it was that change can happen as quickly as the spark of a thought. Resistance to Awakening—resistance to inner truths—keeps us locked in old patterns that do not necessarily benefit our lives, or for that matter, the world. It can leave us disheartened, depressed, and disappointed in ourselves. I was testament to that truth—a place where the webs of time become so thick you cannot see the future. A place where you acclimate to stagnation and you know it, yet do nothing about it.

I closed my eyes and in one of the deepest meditations I had experienced, I sensed this one was different. Emotionally spent yet hopeful, I went in, deep and inward, transcending my own barriers. I was sure I was in there somewhere if but far away, like a distant trumpeter you hope will make a sound so you know you're alive. I had made so many journeys inward in search of the 'I' that this one should have been no different, but I sensed indeed something much different was imminent. Eyes closed, in the darkness, I searched for that lamp that brings light to the soul—the fire of kundalini.

Soon I found my mantra of *Let go of all thoughts good and bad* slid into a prayer of *May the Light of God find me*. It was not a new petition, but in this moment it was far-reaching with spot-on intention and boundless deep compassion for the responsibilities of Spirit. In a matter of minutes I could feel the rise of kundalini stoking a fire deep in the pit. I liken it to the feeling you get when the skies darken and the wind picks up just before the storm. It is like the fragrance that ever-so-briefly fills the air at that precise moment, when you know beyond a shadow of a doubt that it's going to rain. I could *feel* the impending storm of kundalini as its rise shot through my chakras. This happened very quickly. There are no rules for this occurrence as I discovered. It is what it is. I was ready to face the tempest with absolutely no fears. The feeling built in the form of an internal volcano until it erupted through the seventh chakra. This process in Sanskrit is referred to as the *Sahastrara*. I now faced the storm stripped of all my skin. My head felt hollow and before thoughts filled my mind, naked in this chamber, a deep male voice of Spirit—not my own—spoke three words.

"Prepare the vessel."

Upon those words I knew exactly what I needed to do as if I had some magical script written before I was born and now it was being handed to me. I didn't even need to read it. I knew the script. I had to transform my life by becoming celibate, lactovegetarian, doing 24-hour fasts, exercising and eliminating television and newspapers—the latter two a source of over-stimulating the senses and creating fears by others that negatively affect consciousness. The final task I needed to do was sell my house—my beloved home, my temple. This would be difficult emotionally, but was required preparation for my vessel and it felt like I had precious little time to achieve it. I knew from my studies of Buddhism that in the purest sense of becoming Mindful, one must acknowledge that the teacher is not outside you. He is not found in a book. The teacher is inside. The teacher is you. I needed to trust my instincts.

I immediately began this new trek into life the next day, New Year's Day, January 1, 1985. It was the first in a series of the Mindful Teacher's influence and direction. However, 'channeling' is not exactly something an employed scientist announces unless he's professionally suicidal. I had not lost my marbles, and the trusted friends with whom I shared this information didn't think so either.

Before the end of 1985, I realized it was time to quit my work in L.A. and move. I pulled out of various clinical, research and consulting practices. As if these were not big enough changes, one morning I crafted a signpost: 'House for Sale by Owner.' As I placed the wooden stake on the grass preparing to pound the sign in alongside the curb, a car drove up. An Asian man lowered his window, leaned out toward me flopping his elbows over the door, and asked, "Are you selling this house?"

"I am," I confirmed, amazed at the uncanny timing.

"May I come in?" he asked. I walked him through the house. "Perfect!" he said.

He bought it! Within forty-five days I was to move out.

The next phase of the process of *preparing the vessel* was to let go of all possessions. As much as I resisted this notion, I knew it was for the greater good. I held an estate sale with a price tag on everything I owned with only two exceptions: my car and my guitar. By thirty days I had essentially nothing left. For the first time in my adult life, I owned only what would fit into a couple cardboard boxes and two suitcases. The sense of freedom was indescribable. The shackles of ownership, the pride of ego, the self, it was all transforming very quickly.

In the interim of deciding where I'd end up living before I moved to Sedona, if in fact I was even going to move there, my longtime friend and co-scientist Dion offered me a room in his house. I also had a room available as needed in my parent's home in Palm Springs where I often stayed on weekends as I had been pulling out of my audiology posts. Throughout this process, I had also begun building a vision board. The collage was mounted on the wall above my bed in my parent's Palm Springs house.

Slowly, as time went on, I added to the vision board all the dimensions of a woman that I found admirable and desirable and by 1986, the board was almost complete with loving messages I had cut out from magazines I would find; romantic ponderings and gorgeous images from old greeting cards I had saved; many short poems I had written; dried flowers pasted on the board; and dozens of positive affirmations on fortune cookies. It seemed every week I was adding something.

When there was no room left on this two-foot by three-foot poster, I knew the woman represented among all these images was going to be my wife. Quite strikingly dead center in the poster was the stunning black and white image of that woman in slight caricature form clipped from a calendar—long, dense, dark curls flowing down a beautifully sculpted face; captivating eyes; a pure spirit. That's what I wanted. Could I create it?

In yet another meditation on my magic carpet by the fireplace in 1986, I had believed my Mindfulness failed me, and instead, whatever I was trying to focus on at the time melded into a deep and peaceful sleep sitting upright in front of dancing flames. Perhaps it lasted seconds, maybe minutes, I don't know. I was startled out of that ethereal moment as my consciousness reentered the room to the sounds of Gregorian chants. When I opened my eyes I realized that I not only had disappeared from the room, but I had returned with an image stuck in my head—a huge red bell-shaped mountain. This was quite similar to the message 'prepare the vessel' because it functioned like a trigger. I was able to extract truths from the image without the need for words to describe it. From the image in this meditation I 'knew' certain things. I was going to move to the area this image represented, yet, I had never seen this image before. It was as much remarkable as it was odd. It was as if someone had handed me a one-way train ticket with the name of a city on it, one I never heard of, but when I looked at it, I knew, *Ah ha! That's just where I need to go!* The vision was as clear as a bell. In fact, *it was a bell!* I had to trust my intuition.

And so in trusting it, I undertook days of inquiry about a silly bell-shaped red mountain I'd seen in this meditation. Someone eventually remarked, "Oh! That sounds exactly like Bell Rock in Sedona, Arizona!"

I found Sedona on a map and sat there studying it. Why Sedona? Why was Spirit directing me to live there of all the places in the world? After some Internet research, the only answer that evolved was safety.

I was back on the phone asking anyone willing to do so to join me for a trip to visit Sedona. I called Dion.

"Hey! I just discovered this place in Arizona. I know this sounds crazy, but I have this feeling. I believe I may move there. Want to join me to check it out this weekend?"

"How far?"

"Six hours."

"Six hours? Can't do it!" Dion shot back.

I explained my concerns about remaining in California, especially after one of the structural beams in my ceiling had cracked during an earthquake a few years earlier. Dion's wisdom summed up a valuable truth. "I refuse to live my life in fear." I couldn't argue with that. It had also been my thinking—until a greater calling.

I telephoned a second friend, William. He couldn't go either. Then I called Robert. Same response.

Unable to even bribe a friend at this point, I ended up never making the trip. Days went by and I kind of forgot about it. Then exactly two weeks later I got a phone call from the same old friend—the same Robert—late Sunday night.

"Richard! Are you sitting down?" he asked with fever pitch. "Remember you told me about Sedona a couple weeks ago? Well, two days ago, on Friday morning, I was meditating stark raving naked on a boulder at the crest of Mulholland Drive overlooking the Valley, and in the meditation I heard *a male voice!* It wasn't my voice! It said *Go home! Pack your bags! You're moving to Sedona Arizona!* Richard, I was dumbstruck!"

I was equally dumbstruck. Robert wasn't crazy. "This is great, Robert! Let's go out there together. I'll drive!" I insisted. "I'm free this—

"Richard! I already went out there! On Friday!"

"You what?"

"I was guided to buy a house there . . . yesterday! The first house I looked at!"

"You bought . . . *YOU BOUGHT A HOUSE?*"

He did. He gave up his rental apartment, was out of Los Angeles in weeks, and literally transformed his life. He had done in forty-eight hours exactly what I had only been dreaming of doing. I had multiple clinical practices and was heavily entrenched so it was no easy task for me to jump out of L.A. Envious but also proud of Robert for his newfound adventure, as days went into weeks thinking about him, I began feeling like Wile E. Coyote scratching his head wondering where the hell the Roadrunner went.

But soon, time moved as time does and one season fell into another. The vision board collected dust as time passed, and soon I forgot all about those captivating eyes. Another year passed and like the vision board, Sedona just kind of slipped away from consciousness.

It was now September 1987, three month's short of three years of purifying the vessel. I had remained steadfastly on this quest without faltering. As I was leaving Los Angeles to head out to Palm Springs on a Friday evening, on my console was a clipping from a throwaway paper about a professional single's meeting at a hotel in Pasadena—physicians, chiropractors, lawyers, dentists and the like. I would be within one mile of it on the freeway en route to Palm Springs, so I stopped in. I was there no longer than ten minutes, met two lovely women (one in particular named Jo took my breath away) and off alone I went to Palm Springs.

I walked into my bedroom at my parent's place, turned on the light and caught sight of the vision board image of the woman in the center—

there was Jo. Though I hadn't recognized her at the event, I knew Jo was going to be my wife. The vision board was complete.

By then, I had given up all but one of my clinical/research posts for the purpose of clearing the path for the final move. Jo and I fast became a couple and fell madly in love, only for me to learn early-on that she could not leave Los Angeles for another two years until she finished her doctoral dissertation.

In February 1988, she and I took a break to attend the annual gem and mineral show in Tucson. While there, we called my good ol' friend Robert, now well established in Sedona.

"Hey, Jo and I are down here in Tucson and leaving tomorrow. Want some company?"

"It's about time!" he said. "Come on up!"

So off to Sedona we went for the very first time. We came in on Highway 179 during the late afternoon as little mesas came into view. Then riding that one final stretch along the highway finally opened up a vista to the Village of Oak Creek (VOC)—Sedona. What we saw was spellbinding. The stark blue sky contrasted with puffy white clouds and the rising, courtly red rock mountains. I thought it was a Hollywood stage production with the colorations of light and shadowed contrasts. It just didn't look real. The prodigious mountains appeared almost to be props—so majestic in their presence. Jo and I got a chill of excitement through us. We'd never seen anything like this in prior travels to many places in the world.

"Oh my God," Jo uttered. "This is where we're moving!"

I started acting like a scientist. "Come on, honey. We know nothing about this place. No rash decisions."

"Excuse me, my love, weren't you the one who said in your meditation you saw—"

She had such a way of using my own words.

Driving further along Highway 179, there stood Bell Rock. It was its own signpost, shaped like a bell. I was half expecting Rod Serling to step out of the Twilight Zone to start directing traffic. "Over here! Over here! Catch Bell Rock before it lifts off!"

Seeing Bell Rock was a flashback. Maybe this was Spirit's mysterious way of helping us make decisions. We decided since we'd be there for only a night, we'd find a realtor. The first place we stopped, there was Budd. He drove us everywhere looking for open acreage where we could eventually build a house. Nothing materialized.

We drove home the next day a bit dejected. A month later Budd called with a fabulous possibility. You know the feeling you get just before it rains? Jo just knew this was it. She flew out to see the land—acres of pristine virgin wilderness up against national forest. Pines everywhere.

She called me. "This is it honey! We found it! This *is* the land!"

Early in 1990, Jo's longtime friend Laurie was visiting from Los Angeles. We sat meditatively near the last pew of the Chapel of the Holy Cross high on the hill in Sedona. The cool fall breeze through the wide open entry doors blended with the sounds of Gregorian chants, pulling at my ears, tugging at my soul, all familiar sounds and sensations. The many candles lining the sides of the alter flickered and danced in their tall dark red glass containers as though keen to share their secrets, eager to escape—like me.

Laurie suddenly broke the silence, leaning into me, whispering, "You and Jo have to be married in Sedona," she said decisively with a tear rolling off her cheek.

I had not even considered such a thing. Jo and I had already put our deposit down and reserved our place for the wedding back in Los Angeles where most of our friends resided. Almost reflexively I spoke before I thought. "I'm not sure it would be fair to everyone in Los Angeles who'd have to spend a lot of money for hotels to attend our wedding out here."

"They'll come!" Laurie insisted without a blink.

As I pondered her idea, it all felt right. It was one of those 'Sedona moments.' Sedona has gifted millions upon millions of these moments to its trusted visitors. Perhaps they occur to everyone who's been here. It's a moment when time truly stops as you see through your mind's eye with a new vision and understand life in a way you had not imagined. You find yourself *awakening*.

Gusts of the fall breeze shot through the Chapel doorway that day and patted us on the back. My eyes closed and I began slow, rhythmic breathing. My mind filled with music and every cell of my body was at peace. The Chapel was almost completely vacant of visitors, save for those angels that abounded all around us. You could almost hear their voices over the mellifluous sounds of the Gregorian chants.

POSTSCRIPT: Like a crack in a priceless piece of oak, after twenty-five years of aging together, 2012 brought an end to our marriage. However, no matter the history that fostered separation, we have the deepest love, admiration and respect for each other, and a bond for life.

Part IV
Signs, Voices and ETs

"The longest journey is the journey inward."
—Dag Hammarskjöld (second Secretary-General of the United Nations, 1953-1961)

Recent estimates charge that there are 2,000 to 6,000 or more religions and sects on the planet right now. If religions can't seem to agree on the nature of God, love and life, who is to challenge the truth of those who present the deepest of mysteries?

CHAPTER ELEVEN
The Three Signs

Chenoa Miller is currently self-employed as a bookkeeper. In her spare time she enjoys hiking, camping, learning the tarot and all things metaphysical. Chenoa is 39 and has lived in Sedona for seven years.

It was a hot summer day in Austin, Texas in 2004, as my mom and I packed her Toyota Highlander for our road trip to California. We were going to Hemet to help my grandmother move. As we pulled onto the highway, Mom said, "I heard of this spiritual place in Arizona called Sedona, and I was thinking we could stop on our way and check it out."

"Great!" I said.

Little did I know how profoundly this decision would change my life!

Driving down Oak Creek Canyon we were captured by the natural beauty. As we weaved our way through the red rocks of Sedona, I could not have imagined it would be so beautiful. After a nice lunch, we had the best time browsing the little shops, hiking Boynton Canyon and meditating by the creek at Crescent Moon Ranch. But after two days, it was time to drive the scorching six hours to Hemet.

When we finished helping my grandmother pack, we both agreed to spend one more night in Sedona on our trek back to Austin. I spent the day meeting the most amazing people and soaking up the friendly atmosphere of Sedona. On the day we were leaving, something magical happened on the hotel balcony. I was at complete peace with myself and experienced an extraordinary calm in my heart. As I looked out at the beautiful red rocks, suddenly a voice came into my head and told me I was going to move here. Just as quickly a waterfall of blissful tears poured down my face.

I was thrilled, but then reality also kicked in. I had lived in Austin almost all of my thirty years of life and my whole family lived there. This would be a big move for me on my own, not to mention having to quit my job and sell my house before making this monumental shift.

When I got back to Austin the first thing I did was ask the Universe to show me signs if this move would be for my highest good. I had learned that if you get three positive signs, then it's a *yes*.

That day I casually turned over a Sedona magazine that I had brought back and happened to see an ad by Pink Jeep Tours. The words looked up at me in big, bold and bright letters saying, just do it!

That was exciting, but I still needed two more signs. The next day as I was driving to work, I said to myself, "Okay, I'm ready for another sign." One second later I happened to glance toward my left and the driver had her thumb up, like giving the 'thumbs up,' looking straight ahead while driving. I was taken aback, looked again and there she was still driving right beside me, looking straight ahead, her thumb still up in the air! *Wow!* I thought, that's definitely a strange thing for her to do; nevertheless, a positive sign indeed. Now I just needed one more sign.

The very next day I went to work and opened my email. I saw one that I normally would have put straight into my trash folder. However, something told me to open this one and read it. Low and behold, right in front of my face were the words, 'Yes! Yes! Yes!'

Okay okay! I thought with a sigh of relief. I got it! I got the signs! I'm really going to try and do this!

I booked a flight to Phoenix that day to leave the following week. I was tight on money, but I had four days off from work. I would have to find a place to live (specifically two bedrooms, clean, they would have to accept pets, and must have views) and I had to find a job within the four days I was there. I settled into the airplane seat and began reading "The Power of Now" by Eckhart Tolle. An acquaintance of mine just happened to give me the book a couple days before my trip. Every word in the book rang true for me.

I had reserved an economy car at the airport, but when I arrived, they were completely sold out. So they gave me a convertible for the price of the economy car. I did not complain!

With my hair blowing in the wind, radio cranked and a smile on my face, I was in heaven as I again moved among the red rocks and their welcoming open arms. As I settled into the hotel room, I instantly got busy sending my résumé out to as many companies as possible. The next day I sent out more résumés and called several house rentals and apartments. I was getting a little worried because by day three I still hadn't heard back from any jobs and still hadn't found a place to live that suited me. By day four I was beginning to doubt the reliability of my signs. I knew finding a job and a place to live would be the greatest sign because I didn't have the money to come back and do all of this again, and I would have had to give up and stay in Austin.

My plane was leaving Phoenix in just four hours. As I was packing my suitcase, feeling pretty glum, my cell phone rang. It was a company that wanted to interview me in fifteen minutes. I told them I would be right over. After my interview, I was walking to my car when my phone rang again. It was an apartment manager in West Sedona who just happened to have one apartment available. The lady had moved out the day before unexpectedly. He said I could come and look at it right away. My heart raced as I sped over there. It was a two-bedroom, spacious, clean apartment with the best views in the complex, and they accepted pets! As I was viewing the apartment, my phone rang again and it was the company that I had just interviewed with. They told me I got the position and wanted to know when I could start! I put down a deposit for the apartment and told the company I could start in three weeks!

My convertible and I lost track of the two-hour drive back to the

Phoenix airport. It felt like only five minutes and somehow, possibly with the help of the vortexes, I made my plane on time. I was ecstatic on the flight home, but one more obstacle had to be surmounted.

I had to put my house on the market. I had a cute and cozy three-bedroom house, but it needed some work before I could sell it, and I only had about two weeks to fix it up with very little money to do so. I decided to put my manifesting skills to work. The siding on my house was very worn and chipped, and I knew that I couldn't sell it in this shape. I started to visualize my house with brand new siding. I didn't put any limitations or negative energy toward this, I just knew with all of my soul that I had new siding on my house. Within two days, I received a call from my stepdad saying that he just helped put new siding on a friend's home and they had exactly enough left over to do my entire house—for free! And on top of that, it was hardy board siding, the most expensive you can get!

"Bring it on!" I said. "Perfect!"

Now, the next thing I needed was a new bathroom vanity. I visualized a new vanity in my bathroom for as cheap as possible. I then went to Home Depot and right before my eyes was the perfect size $200 vanity on sale for $50.

I also had to paint the cabinets, clean the house and pack all of my stuff, and had less than two weeks to do it. My friend, who's a painter, came and painted the cabinets very inexpensively and I had a slew of friends and family that helped me clean and pack. I felt blessed.

One week before I was to leave, my 10 year-old dog Utah started having a harder time walking. His hips had been giving out for a while, but seemed to be getting so much worse. I loved Utah as anyone would love a cherished member of the family. I grew so worried about how my friend could make the very challenging 1100-mile trip to Sedona. I decided to take him to the vet again, because he looked like he was in so much pain. As I was getting him out of the car, he collapsed in the parking lot. I got help to carry all seventy pounds of him into the vet's office. The decision was made to put him to sleep to relieve his pain. The vet left me alone with Utah for a few minutes. Through my tears, before he passed, he looked up at me. I could read his eyes. "It's okay," he was saying. "I'm ready to go, but we'll be together again." I watched as my precious, sweet and trusted buddy passed, and with his passage came the awareness he was giving up his life to allow me to more freely continue my journey.

In an unusual situation of coincidence, only a matter of four days later, my beloved 14 year-old cat also died by getting attacked by three dogs that sneaked out of their yard that day. After getting over the shock of losing my precious pets, it dawned on me that I would be moving to Sedona without any animal companions. Then, right before I left Austin, the Universe brought a cat into my life. My aunt called me and said the most beautiful long-haired cat walked onto her property a week earlier, and none of the neighbors knew where he came from. She posted signs, but no one claimed him. I drove to her house and immediately fell in love with Willow—his new name. On the drive to Sedona, Willow sat on my lap and purred, and didn't complain the entire way. I still have him to this day and he has fit into my life like we've known each other forever.

POSTSCRIPT: Since I moved here, my mother, my grandmother and my aunt all moved here from Austin, and they love it too. I've made friends with so many amazing people and have learned so much from living here. I believe if you have an open heart and mind, some manifesting skills, and are aware of the signs around you, the Universe will show you the way. I found mine . . . Sedona.

CHAPTER TWELVE
The Labyrinth

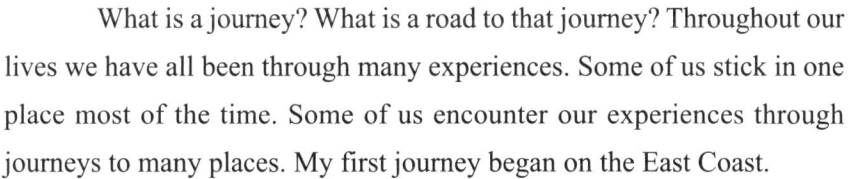

Janet Feeney was the Third Place Winner with the following essay submitted to the Mystical Sedona Stories Writing Contest.® She is a wide collector of crystals, does readings from your own personal rock which she also can help select, and does extensive numerology delineations that incorporate channelings based on an individual's unique numbers. Janet does tarot, medicine wheel, labyrinth walks and rituals. She's 61, enjoys writing poetry, and has lived in Sedona for fourteen years.

What is a journey? What is a road to that journey? Throughout our lives we have all been through many experiences. Some of us stick in one place most of the time. Some of us encounter our experiences through journeys to many places. My first journey began on the East Coast.

I grew up in Greenwich Village, New York. I was raised by my mother's side of the family. A very large family. My grandmother was Polish and my grandfather was Ukrainian. My aunts married into Irish and Italian families, some of whom were involved with the mob. And gambling. My grandparents owned a restaurant on the Hudson River. Cargo ships would come from Portugal and other faraway places where they'd dock on the river directly across from the restaurant. The deckhands were always familiar faces who would eat at the restaurant. Many times when the restaurant closed, grandpa would hold late night card games in the back. Grandma would make snacks for the cigar-smoking men. Here they were: the Portuguese, the Italians, the Russians, the Polish, the Irish—and me. Oh, and the cops. Because we were mobster-friendly related, my family also had a strong relationship with the police. I was a good kid. I never got into trouble. How could I? I had my father's Irish last name!

Often I would hear stories of faraway lands and people. Stories that were filled with excitement and danger, and odd tales with unexplained endings where people were saved by mysterious persons who would just come out of the woodwork—like Angels or something. And strange rocks glowing in the dark. And mysterious shadows. And true-to-the-end pets. And how to pray, the right way. I learned from the git-go how to keep my eyes open all around my head, how to read people who I knew or didn't know, how to understand energy. How to use energy. About protection and guidance and living on my own. And that I was never really alone.

Throughout my life I've travelled to many places and learned many things. I met my father at age 13 and went to live with him in Anaheim, California until I was 19. At age 21, I travelled across the states, meeting people from all over, getting to 'know myself.' Later I joined the U.S. Army just because I wanted to live in Europe. I lived in Germany for nearly two years. My obsession for 'Life' became my life. I met people from all over the world and soon discovered what 'picking up on energy' meant. Back then, still anchored in the Village, I bought my first crystal. It was a three-inch tall green quartz with a tiny brass frog perched on its ledge, sitting on an acrylic square base.

One night while walking in the city I came across an occult shop. I hadn't any idea what that meant, yet I was curious. I don't know why I felt so nervous. I suppose I was afraid someone I knew would see me standing there, yet I walked in anyway, very quickly. It was all so new and spooky. Most likely I was unaware of having my first empathic experience. I bought my very first book on magic and I kept it hidden until I left New York for Southern California. My interest in rocks and spooky books waned.

It is 1973. I was 23 years old when I moved back to Southern California, living in a huge house with six other hippies. All of a sudden, I had this unique urge to study palms and the tarot. I don't know why.

I bought my first books. I studied ardently and did my first readings on my dear friend Luella. She believed in me and my new interest (two Scorpios), yet was skeptical at best. During the tarot reading I read her future, because I quite distinctly remember some months later she told me that it was weird that the man I told her she was going to meet not only came into her life when I said he would, he also fit the description I gave to a tee, and that I said they would move in together, and they did! When Luella told me of the materialization of my prediction, she not only walked away pretending it wasn't freaking her out, she mentioned I should do readings. I passed it off mainly because I hadn't any idea what the heck a reading really was, and I also became intimidated because I really felt I knew nothing at all.

And this, like the green crystal and the magic book, was put to the wayside. But hey! Now I could read palms, do tarot readings, and I owned a real crystal that sat on a shelf next to a book on magic!

There isn't any doubt that during the course of our lives we're learning from everything we do, from every person we meet, from every challenge that will take us to our next lesson. The Universe knows so much better than we can ever know what our next step is, where we are to go next. So much energy from the places and people we meet is absorbed with our own energies.

After Southern Cal came the Army experience. Then Europe. After being discharged I was back and forth from the east coast to the west coast, winding up in San Francisco. I just couldn't settle.

There I began to study magic in all its forms. San Francisco moved me to Santa Fe, New Mexico for five years in the mid-1980s. The metaphysical world began its reappearance. I recall the first day I had gone to town to look around. I walked by a crystal shop and was pulled inside like a magnet to iron with no idea why. Again. I really hadn't any interest. Yet, I was absolutely amazed at the stunning displays of rocks. Behind a locked window cabinet were some beautiful amethysts of various sizes.

They were pretty expensive. However, one stood out at the very top that was larger than an open hand, with a sticker price of five dollars.

I got the salesman's attention and said, "I want to purchase that particular rock please."

When he saw the price, his face rearranged. He inspected the rock and the price. "You got to be kidding," he said.

However, he was obligated to make good on the sticker price as marked. Today this amethyst sits here in Sedona several inches away from the green crystal I purchased in NYC. Friends o'mine. It was in Santa Fe that I took up avid study of Numerology, of which, to this day, is my forte.

After those glorious five years in Santa Fe, I moved to Phoenix. During this period of time I began doing readings. Words just poured out of my mouth. It just came naturally, and that's all I ever thought about it (except that it amazed others). I never gave it a second thought. I just considered that it was my thing to do. One time on a job at Union Bank, I was having a conversation about metaphysics. The lady said to me "You should go to Sedona." I didn't even know what a Sedona was.

The employment at Union Bank ended and I was having a very difficult time finding work. All of a sudden, like the wind at your back, I began taking a deep, deep interest in the various areas of metaphysics. I studied numerology, Reiki, crystals, A Course in Miracles, Alice Bailey, the stars. You name it. I started seeing things like ghosts and shadows. I began going to the library very often and would stay up to the wee hours of the morning studying everything I could get my hands on.

This went on for quite a long time. I began experiencing out of the ordinary happenings that were demonstrating exceptional powers on my part. There wasn't any preparation, so to speak, with this newfound gift. It just started to happen. During my studies, I frequently requested only Truth from the Universe and inner knowledge that I could recognize as Truth. In conversations with people I would 'hear' at a higher level of consciousness.

This became a period where I couldn't find any work—anywhere. Not even at temporary agencies. I was mainly broke, living on food stamps and government assistance, and facing an eviction notice. But I fought the eviction to the bitter end. I wasn't leaving my little study sanctuary called home, albeit the curiosity I had with the metaphysical arena continued to build. I studied the Universe, other dimensions, angels, demons, Kabala, and so much more. Once I realized I had so much more to learn, I decided to relocate back to Santa Fe where there were many metaphysical schools. I needed to find out how and where I fit into this newly found spiritual arena.

The landlord gave me back my deposit in full. I put all the belongings that I wanted to keep into storage and sold everything else in a final month-long garage sale. I bought a bus ticket and by the end of the month I was on my way to Santa Fe.

In Santa Fe I didn't have a car, but now they had bus transportation, so I took public bus transit everywhere. I stayed with a friend in a fancy mobile home park residence until I could get my own place. I began to research various schools, visiting them and asking questions. I was trying to find my niche. I found out that I could volunteer at conferences and seminars and thereby be admitted for free. I was on a roll. Little did I know I would only be in Santa Fe for six weeks.

One day while shopping at a co-op I noticed a flyer posted on the community wall inviting volunteers to help build a labyrinth in the grove at Frenchy's Park. I took great interest and volunteered. (I knew what a labyrinth was because of one on the floor in the back of a church in San Francisco. It was designed into a huge carpet. It was donated from a church in Scotland. I had a great interest in it and walked the labyrinth a lot.) A labyrinth is a large circle of continuous paths representing your Self and your journeys through Life. It's usually mapped out on the ground with large stones that mark seven continuous paths in a diameter of roughly 45-

50 feet where the center represents an altar. At one point there's an entrance. As you slowly begin the path around, you're also entering your Being within. At this point, your space becomes sacred. Here you reflect upon your Life, the people you've met, the choices you've made. You begin to release the negative and integrate what you know to be the positive. For many, it is a prayer. As you progress toward the center, you're detaching from the past all that has bothered you or held you back, and you release it. At the center you contemplate your walk and what you've learned from it. You meditate on your purpose there and feel the goodness within yourself. It's a good custom to put something into or onto the Earth as a gift—a crystal, rock, flower, coin, a piece from a tree. You leave it on top or bury it. Now you begin your path walking out. You should bring back with you something from the center. It's all energy. It's an exchanging reminder that we are all One. The journey consists of inner reflection of what you would give to the world (for example, Peace), to the people (Love), and to the Earth (Blessings and Healings). You must leave with Peace, Love and Blessings for your Self, too. As you exit the labyrinth you become One again with your outer world and you go in Peace.

So, in Santa Fe, one-hundred signatures were needed to bring to City Hall for approval. The signatures were obtained, the approval was granted and a date was set up to begin to build this labyrinth. The men picked up the hay, they got the hoses to water down the ground, they dug the ground to make the circle, then loaded and unloaded rocks from trucks. They built an entrance trellis, worked hard and did all that was needed to make this happen.

The women managed designing the labyrinth circle and placing rocks all around the periphery. We taught the children how to help and explained why they were doing what they were doing. We built an altar in the middle of the circle. I taught some of the children how to empower crystals and how to bury them in the ground and the reasons for Blessings.

We drew empowerment from the surrounding forest, and a small group that formed a band played music all day as we worked.

At lunch, it was a feast of pot-luck natural organic health foods. There were a lot of dishes that were unfamiliar. I'm a city girl! I brought fruit and potato chips. The kids and the guys mad-dashed for the chips. I should have brought more!

Except for all the many months of studying metaphysics and applying as much as I could through hands-on experiences, I was very much a novice at it. I was attending seminars. I began seeing healing lights of gold. I was having 'crazy' dreams. I was manifesting stuff really fast and I seemed to be learning at an accelerated pace.

We were done near sunset and had our first ritual. The labyrinth was completed start to finish in one day. It was awesome to be part of such a ceremony. When the sun set, we packed up and everyone went their separate ways.

A couple of weeks had passed and by now I had two jobs. The first job I had was waitressing at Red Lobster, and I was making up to and over $40-$100 a night in tips. I remember when I received my first paycheck I heard Spirit say to hold onto the check. Listening to that message, I put the check away in my suitcase that was stored under my friend's bed. I put it out of my mind, forgetting all about it until one particular afternoon.

I had just finished working at my second job and was at a bus transfer point waiting for the next bus to arrive. It began to drizzle on and off, and it was taking a long time for the next bus to arrive. I got up and walked around to bide my time. No bus. I sat and waited. No bus. I strolled around in the drizzle. No bus. Then I looked over to my far right and there was Frenchy's Park. *Hmmm,* I thought. I had a strong passion to walk the labyrinth. So what if the bus comes? I've waited this long I could wait longer. So I went across to the park, walked down the grove and stood at the trellis that marked the entrance to this newly built labyrinth.

I slowly did my walk about and offered passionate prayers at the altar. I recalled the day we all gathered to build that circle. I was beginning to feel at home in Santa Fe once again, yet still somewhat detached. Like what was I really doing there and what was going to happen next? I thought about the energies I was feeling every day and every night from the mountains—the Sangre de Cristo (the Blood of Christ). Each day when I awoke and went outside I could feel and hear the mountains moaning. The same thing happened in the evening when the sun set blazing reds across the face of the mountains. Santa Fe wasn't the quiet small town it used to be from the last time I had been there some ten years earlier. The outer end had turned into a huge shopping mall and now there were busses for transportation versus just cars or taxis. I yearned to know where I really belonged. I yearned for the same solid ground on which the mountain stood. I was blazing with Life, but didn't know which direction to blaze.

When I reached the end of the walk, I stood there and asked the Universe: "What now?" I was standing in the grove at the trellis. It was very, very still and quiet. Suddenly, out of nowhere, I heard a soft yet deep male voice say, "Go to Sedona." It scared the hell out of me. It spoke from behind my head. I turned very quickly in back of me, first to my left, then to my right. Then to my right and left again. I was the only one there!

I suddenly ran to the top of the grove to see who was playing with my head. Perhaps it was one of the people I was with building the labyrinth. Yet there wasn't anyone around. I stood there alone in the park. Suddenly, I heard a loud rattling noise. On my left and out of nowhere came a girl barreling past me on what looked like an old Schwinn bicycle. She was pedaling so fast she just shot right past like a thunderbolt! She must have been about 11 years old. I looked again to my left wondering from where she had appeared. Then, as I glanced to my right to watch her, she had disappeared! Gone! I was alone in the park again. No rattling bicycle noise, no wind blowing in my ears, just me and the rainy drizzle.

Frenchy's Park is a people and pet park. All the time. Every day. People came to walk their dogs in the morning, in the rain, in the wind, in the sun. This day there wasn't anyone around. Elderly people come to sit on benches to just sit, but they weren't there. Kids come and play ball. There weren't any kids. The park also was marked with many gopher holes. I didn't see one gopher the whole time I was there. This was getting spooky. I just put it aside that the little girl on the bike lived in the neighborhood and knew the hills in the park and just took a shortcut down a hill and disappeared out of sight.

Brimming with curiosity, I went back down the grove and stood at the opening and thought about what had just happened—voice, bike and all. It was quiet and eerie.

I uttered some guttural sound, "Hmphh!" Then I took a deep breath and directed my attention to the voice I had heard. I timidly mumbled, "Okay—what did you say?"

The voice over my shoulder was soft, deep and male. Again it said, in a slow, forceful calm, "Go to Sedona," as if that is what I had to do right then, there and now! No ifs, ands or buts.

All of a sudden I could feel my solar plexus burst open and was overcome by a sensation of joy I had never felt before. It felt so good it hurt. I started to laugh and I started to cry, all at the same time. I ran to the forest on my right and hugged the first tree I came to. I thanked it and I thanked God and I thanked the Universe! I now <u>knew</u> where I was going! Even though I still didn't know what 'Sedona' really was.

I ran up the hill. I could see the bus coming to the bus stop. I hustled. I got on board to be let off at the mobile home courtyard entrance where I was staying with my friend—in Santa Fe.

As soon as I got off the bus, my friend drove into the courtyard. She had a co-worker in the car and was driving her home. However, she was making a pit stop to the house first. She picked me up to go to the house. I was laughing and couldn't stop and really didn't know why.

It was nearing 5:00 p.m. Everything that happened next happened in precise clockwork with no stops in between. I went to get the Red Lobster paycheck that I had saved and now knew the reason I had secreted it away. It was to pay for my fare to Sedona. The tip money I saved to get an apartment was now going to be my expense money for my new journey. I made a mad dash outside about to take a 15-minute walk to the bus stop when my friend said she would take me to the bus stop.

When we got there, the bus was just arriving. "Wow! Good timing," she said.

Pleasantly enough, the clouds broke up and the sun began shining through with a rainbow! I took the bus to the transfer depot to get on a bus that would take me to the bank before it closed at five. It was Friday. The transfer bus arrived as soon as I did. I got to the bank seven minutes before closing time. When I was done, I waited for the next bus that would take me back to the depot to get a bus to the Santa Fe Greyhound Bus Station where I would purchase my ticket to Sedona. Needless to say, that bus arrived immediately, and at the transfer depot, the bus to the Greyhound Station pulled up right behind it.

As I walked into the Santa Fe Greyhound Bus Station, the man behind the counter looked up at the clock. It was 5:45 p.m. I was the only customer there. It was a small place.

"One ticket to Sedona, Arizona—one way," I requested.

He looked at me and smiled. "You have very good timing because we close at six o'clock. And you're also very lucky because there's only one ticket left to your destination from Santa Fe."

I started wondering if there really was a Sedona, that maybe these past few hours were something out of my imagination. But no—that voice was absolutely real and clear. I wasn't imagining anything. I got my ticket, went home to pack, and two days later I was on my way to Sedona.

When I arrived at the Flagstaff Greyhound Bus Station, I spent nearly one hour on the pay phone trying to find a way to get to Sedona without spending an arm and a leg. No busses, no shuttles, no inexpensive cabs. Finally, I discovered Mark driving a taxi. He was friendly and funny and only charged me $40. About three months later while I was walking along Highway 89A, someone shouted my name. It was Mark waving his arm at me from his cab with a big smile on his face.

"Hi ya, Mark!" I yelled back."

We have never crossed paths since then, yet I still have his card in my wallet.

Back on August 22, 1998 when Mark's taxi pulled into the Sedona Hostel that once existed on Brewer Road, up a block from where Burger King still stands, three young guys got up from the picnic table, ran into the driveway and unloaded my bags out of the trunk as if they were expecting my arrival. The lady, Carol, who managed the hostel, walked up to me and said, "Sweetie, you're lucky, because there's only one bed left!" Then she looked at me with an embracing smile and said, "Welcome home!"

POSTSCRIPT: It is here in Sedona where I discovered I'm a channel.

CHAPTER THIRTEEN
The Encounter

Kia-Dawn Davenport was born and raised in Philadelphia. She worked as a paramedic for the Philadelphia Fire Department for fifteen years and retired in June, 2011. She is proud of two grown daughters and six grandchildren and has lived in Sedona for about eighteen months.

A little over 18 months ago I lived in Philadelphia, PA. I was saving lives, but the task was grueling working as a paramedic for 911—the fire department. I used to love the job, but about ten years into it I began to feel so burned out over the gunshots, heart attacks, car accidents, overdoses, death, and so on. However, I did like delivering babies. They have such a wonderful energy, and the parents were usually happy. Everyone else who called 911 was usually so stressed out, sick, crying, in pain, angry, dying, bleeding! I was working two ten-hour days followed by two fourteen-hour nights and then there was overtime. I was one of only a few black women in the department although the numbers were increasing. It was very stressful all the way around—the job, the people, the city, my life.

This story starts about five years earlier. I had an online bookstore for spiritual and self-help books, started with my at-the-time boyfriend. I love books and had already done ten years in the fire department so I was thinking of a retirement plan. We started the online bookstore together and named it Inner Journey Books.

Things were not going well, trying to start the business, working and trying to maintain my relationship with my boyfriend/business partner which was the typical story of how he just wanted to be friends, not get married. At the time I didn't mind. I was a single parent of two daughters as well, one of whom still lived at home.

I must say I loved my bookstore. I worked on that website in my spare time, which tended to be about four hours each day. I was very proud of it. It was somehow soothing and a de-stressor, getting the accounts and picking out the books that would help people and putting everything online, answering the emails and handling the small number of customers we did made me feel good. I did most of the work, but that was okay because my boyfriend was a good financial partner and went half on all our business expenses which was very helpful.

One night I went to sleep after a hard day of work and began to dream. I don't remember the dream, but when I awoke, a voice was in my head. It said, "You need to move to Sedona." That was all. Only thing was, I had never heard of Sedona. Couldn't tell you where it was. I didn't think much about it, just the remnants of some forgotten dream. I threw the thought out of my mind and got ready for work, no time to eat, have to go save lives—hurry! I was always rushing.

I showered, brushed my teeth, combed my hair, put on my uniform, ran downstairs, got in the car and took off rushing to a place I did not want to be anymore. On my way I was caught behind a slow moving truck, pissed, I honked my horn. The driver paid me no mind. I sat there cursing under my breath, and then I noticed something on the back of the truck, the logo said Arizona Ice Tea. All I thought was I hate iced tea.

The thing about that particular station I was working at that day was that the squad does not go into effect until 8:00 a.m. So you better be on time. I was two minutes late because of that truck. Of course, it had nothing to do with the fact that I left the house at the last minute! I pulled up racing. My lieutenant was standing outside the station as well as a few of the firemen, all shaking their heads at my tardiness. The lieutenant pointed to the squad, my partner was sitting in the passenger seat and flipped the lights on just as I got out of my car. We had a call and it was my turn to drive. No time for coffee, it was the beginning of another day of rushing through the city, lights and sirens blaring, the sick and dying depending on us.

When I pulled up on the scene, the police were standing outside of a locked minivan in the middle of the street as if they had stopped for the red light and never moved when the light changed. The car was a Kia Sedona. I stopped just in back of it. For a moment I just stared at it suddenly recalling the voice. Being that my name is Kia, I thought, *that's odd!*

Maybe I had dreamed about getting this car in my dream. I looked at it. I didn't like the car, mine was better. Again I threw the thought out of my head. The person locked in the car was a diabetic who went down at the wheel waiting for the light to change—foot still on the brake. The police got the door open and put the car in park. I went to work.

I got through the day, no problems. Once home I talked to my boyfriend on the phone. He told me of a Mind Body and Soul Expo at the Valley Forge Convention Center. I thought that would be great, we could go and promote our bookstore. Possibly get some new accounts to sell something other than books. I had wanted to expand and sell classes and maybe some tours to sacred places. We bought the tickets online. The thought of Sedona was long gone.

Two weeks passed and it was time to go to the expo. There were many exhibits there. Two of them caught my eye. One was a booth where a couple was selling medicinal-grade essential oils. We stopped and listened to the spiel. They let us smell the oils—they were fabulous! I thought this would be great to add to our store, I could put a whole section in for them. I talked to the owner of the business. I told him about our website and our small company, asked about drop shipping. He was more than happy to let us sell his products. He'd give us wholesale prices and drop ship, but there was one catch. We had to take an aromatherapy class.

I talked it over with my boyfriend as we both had vacations coming up and I thought we could fit it in. We went back to the vender's table. As the expo was in Pennsylvania, I just assumed that the week-long class would also be in Pennsylvania. For some reason, I even thought it would be in Philadelphia. We agreed to take the class. *Aromatherapy-1 sign us up!* He told us all about it, the dates fit into our coming vacations. Great. Then he told us where it was—Sedona!

The word flashed me right back to the morning I had the thought, *You need to move to Sedona!* I just stared at the man. I asked, "Did you say Sedona?"

"Yes." He answered, "Sedona, Arizona."

He handed me his brochure. I saw the red rocks on the brochure. They were like remnants of a dream I could not remember. Through my haze I could still hear him talking, "You'll love it there it's beautiful. I live just outside of Sedona. The class is at my house."

The rest of what he said was a blur. All I could think was that this is crazy. I had never even heard of this place and now I was going to take a class there. The class was a few months later in the summer. A month before we were supposed to go I came across a book I wanted to sell on my site. I looked up the author's website. Come to find out he also gave sacred tours and he and his wife gave classes on various metaphysical studies. I thought this is great if I could get his account and sell not only his books but also the sacred tours and classes. This was just what I had been looking for. As I did the research I found he did four tours—Egypt, Peru, somewhere in England and Sedona vortexes.

I thought *What is it with this Sedona thing?* I attempted to contact him. He did not respond to my business inquiries. So I decided to contact him using my own name instead of my business name and see if I could get a tour to the vortexes in Sedona since I had no idea what a Sedona vortex was and I was going to be there anyway in the next month. Secretly I thought I'd take the two-day tour and talk to him in person and get the account.

This time he did respond. He said he would do a tour just for me since he lived in Sedona. Although normally he would not have done it because it was in August and it was too hot to do a tour, but he said that something told him to make an exception.

Everything was set. We were going to Sedona on a business trip. A couple of weeks before it was time to go my boyfriend attempted to bail on the trip. He said we should go take a real vacation somewhere nice. I said, "You can't do that, this is business and we have already paid for everything."

He just didn't want to go and tried to talk me out of it, saying we could just get the money back and go have some much needed fun instead. Finally I said, "You don't have to go, but I'm going, I don't do business like that, we have got to get some new accounts. I'm going for it with or without you."

It just seemed the closer we got to the date, the more excited I became. I had to go! He couldn't believe I wanted to go there instead of to the Caribbean. But I did. It seemed I was being called there. I wanted to see what it was about. I kept remembering the voice I heard in my head that morning. I was intrigued.

So the date came. We drove all the way from Philadelphia to Sedona. It took us three days! I didn't mind. It was a great road trip and we really got to know each other even better on the ride. It was the first time I had spent that much time with him since we didn't live together.

I must say I have been to a few places, the Caribbean, Jamaica, Egypt and other places in the U.S., but never experienced what I experienced on that trip. We got to Sedona and everything was fine. It was beautiful—outstandingly so. But that was not what got my attention. I was mostly concerned with the class I had taken and getting the new accounts. I was only vaguely interested in the vortexes.

On the second day after we arrived we went on the vortex tour.

Everything started okay. We met our guide and he took us up a mountain. I think it was someplace around Bell Rock. We all talked as we walked. It was hot. He explained about vortex energy and asked if we could feel it. I did not. I must say my mind was really on how to break into a conversation about my website and trying to get this contract.

We climbed higher. I was tired and hot. At a flat area our guide told us to stop and he laid down a large blanket for us to lie on. My boyfriend and I laid on it. He gave us something to hold in our hands and said for us to close our eyes and relax for about 15 minutes and then tell him what we saw. In the meantime he said a few words that I didn't quite catch. He touched my head and my chest. He said he was clearing us. I thought to myself, *Clearing us of what?* But I said nothing. He put on music from a little CD player that he had (flute and drums). We laid there with our eyes closed.

After a few moments I felt very relaxed, almost as if I was floating. Even the music seemed to fade away. I heard someone quietly call my name. At first I thought it was the guide. I thought maybe I had fallen asleep and that it was time to go. So I turned my head in the direction of the voice and opened my eyes.

There were two people standing there next to me. I suppose I could say people, although *beings* was probably a better word. They were green. Thin green people. I had never seen anything like them. One was very tall and made of simply green light. The other was very short, made of the same green glowing light although it was slightly wider than the other one. I couldn't take my eyes off of them. They motioned for me to come with them. I turned to look at my boyfriend who lay beside me oblivious to these beings, his eyes closed. The guide was sitting under a tree not far away fiddling with something in his backpack.

Again they motioned for me to come. The tall one spoke, which I thought was odd because it did not have a mouth. I could hear the voice in my head. The same voice I had heard months ago telling me to move to Sedona—a familiar voice, a soothing voice. "It's alright, come, there is nothing but peace, no fear, come, we want to show you something." The short one motioned again for me to come with them.

I felt no fear from them, just a soothing peace. I knew I would be safe with them and that I should go. So I got up from the blanket and stood with them for a moment. They both briefly looked me up and down, as I was doing the same with them. I didn't ask them any questions, although I'm not quite sure why. I just found them both fascinating. Their hands didn't have the correct number of digits and they had no fingernails, but this was not frightening.

Their eyes were huge and deep as pools and there was no white in them, just huge deep dark almond-shaped pools. They wore no clothes or shoes, and had no body hair or genitals that I could detect. They simply glowed that florescent green as if they were made of green light.

I don't know why I was so fearless! Strange as it sounds it seemed I knew them somehow, but hadn't seen them in a long time. Suddenly, I was glad to see them. It seemed okay so I went with them. We began to walk, one on each side of me. I wondered where we were going. The short one pointed ahead of us about a hundred yards away. There was a building that hadn't been there before. At least I hadn't seen it, although I don't know how I could have missed it.

It was a huge pyramid shaped building gleaming white. I had the feeling it was a temple. As we got closer I realized it had no windows or doors. This was a little puzzling. I wondered how we would get in, and why had I not noticed this before. They both touched me easing me forward. I felt a slight electric sensation go through my body upon their touch that made me feel light as a feather. With their hands on me we walked right through the wall.

Once inside I looked around. There was nothing in there. No

furniture at all, just the gleaming white walls of a single room. The tall one motioned for me to follow. I followed behind to the center of the room. A metallic table appeared there. I guess that is my best description of it, although it was flat it had no legs holding it up. It was just suddenly floating there in the middle of the room. I was told to lay on it, which I did.

The short one came to my side and waved a long fingered hand over my forehead. As soon as this was done a scanner appeared above my head. I don't know why I called it that, but that was what popped into my head as this device moved above me down to my feet and then back up to my head and then disappeared just as quickly. I felt as if I had been scanned with a white light.

Still I was not afraid.

The short one told me to sit up and look. I did what I was told and looked forward toward the wall beyond my feet where a projection was beginning to show on the wall. I stared at it fascinated. It was me. I lived in Sedona. I had many new friends. I was having a house warming party it seemed. I was in my new house, in my backyard greeting the people that were coming in through the house outside to where the party was being held. I did not know these people, but I did in this projection. I knew them and we all were friends. They were proud of me. I had accomplished something although I do not know what.

I was showing them a mountain. It was a beautiful view from my backyard. A mountain I had never seen before. Not one of the many red mountains, it was sort of beige. I was later to find it was called Thunder Mountain. I was very happy. All the stress I normally felt was gone.

Previously I had not been a very happy person. I was a loner except for my boyfriend, a single parent, stressed out by life and work. I helped those I had come in contact with, because I was helped by strangers when I was young—a runaway from an abusive home. I had lived in many foster and group homes growing up and had many trust and anger issues. But in this projection of me I was happy, had friends, my children were grown and gone—they had not moved here with me. I was free of my issues, happy and loved.

I looked more closely. Yeah, it was me all right, without that mean, serious, stressed-out look on my face. I turned, puzzled and looked at the beings standing next to me. Why were they showing me this? What did it mean? They both gestured toward the wall with the projection before me. I could hear them in my mind.

"This could be your life if you choose. We want to show you what could be if you wish it. This is your home. We have called you here to show you this. You have things to do here that will help many, a different life that will bring you joy. There is a job for you to do."

I stared at the projection and was amazed. I appeared truly happy and at ease. I asked, "What is it I'm supposed to do?"

The images faded from the wall. There was a moment of silence. I asked again, "What is it I'm to do?"

They motioned for me to stand up from the table I had been sitting on. It was time to go back. "You will find out when and if you come. You will know. This is all we are to show you. You must make the choice."

Somewhere inside I knew not to ask any more questions. We left the building the same way we entered. They walked me back to the blanket, I sat down and they were gone. I looked up and the building was gone as well.

Our guide was napping and my boyfriend lay where I had left him. In my hand was the round metal ball I had been given to hold by the guide. Just then he woke and came over to me. He asked what we had seen. My boyfriend said he saw colored balls floating before him the whole time and that he was soothed by the brilliant colors.

I explained to them both what I had seen. My boyfriend said I must have fallen asleep and had a dream. He was a little upset that he wasn't in it. The guide tried to explain something about dimensions, time and space, that they did not exist. That this was a sacred place and long ago other beings lived here and that the temple was actually still here although very few people are allowed to see it. That I must be very special to have not only seen it, but was invited to go inside of it. To be honest I did not know what to think.

It took me another five years to get to Sedona after this experience, because my boyfriend asked me to wait for him to retire and we would be married and move here. In the meantime, my youngest daughter grew up and left home. I broke up with my boyfriend, and lost my online bookstore as well. I have reflected on this experience many times, although I don't tell anyone about it because I figure they would just think I was crazy or that it was a dream. It was not.

Last year almost to the date, I retired from the 911 system, sold my house, bought a BMW and moved to Sedona—alone. I arrived on the 3rd of July 2011, making Independence Day my first full day living here. I rent a small place and am still confused about what I am to be doing here. I am no longer stressed and am getting over my issues. I have met friends, good people, friends that I never thought I would have. To say the least, I love it here. I go for hikes and try to find the place that I saw the temple—*the beings*. I don't ask to see them, but occasionally I look. Once I was on a mountain and heard a voice come from the rock that said to me, "What took you so long? I've been waiting for you."

POSTSCRIPT: I'm in awe of Sedona even as I sit writing at this very moment. I often wonder, as I know I will move at some point to my own house, if it will be with a view of Thunder Mountain. I wonder what it is I'm supposed to do. Currently where I live the red rocks surround me except for the one side where I can see Thunder Mountain from a treehouse in the yard where I'm writing right now. I'm not rich. I retired at only 47 years old, so my pension is small, but I'm happier than I've ever been. At some point I'll work again—some small job, doing what, I have no idea. It doesn't really matter. I'm here. I'm home.

Part V
Love Stories

"A journey of a thousand miles begins with a single step."
– Lao Tzu

There is nothing more powerful than the union of two people to bring the most profound connection through love. So often we hear that someone was in exactly the right place at the right time or it could not have happened. The *single step* that puts one at the intersection of another's life is considered by some to be pure luck, by others as coincidence, and a few consider it a miracle.

CHAPTER FOURTEEN
A Love Story

Karoline Grant is a Freefall Certified Empowerment Coach, Journey Practitioner and Massage Therapist. She loves to see people overcome their limitations and reclaim their power to live a richer, more rewarding life, one that provides a greater sense of freedom, well-being, joy, inner peace and abundance. Karoline is 47 and has lived in Sedona for one year. [www.karolinestevens.com]

Sometimes life has a way of really shaking a person up and getting her to do the unexpected. Well that is literally what happened to me a year ago February. Originally from Germany, I had been living and working in Christchurch, New Zealand for the previous twenty years and had no plans to leave. February 22, 2011 was a lovely, sunny Tuesday. It's just so beautiful there, looking out over the estuary and the ocean to one side and the city and mountains to the other. So picturesque! Summer in Christchurch is hard to beat.

I was excited because my mum had just come over from Germany to spend a few weeks with me. We were preparing to go into the city center because I had some client appointments in my coaching and massage clinic and my mum was planning to visit a travel agent on the 14th floor of a high-rise building to extend her ticket.

All of a sudden, there was a tremendous rumbling noise and the second floor of the house began to move like a leaf in the wind! It felt like someone had picked up the house and was shaking it violently from side to side. Cupboard doors crashed on the right, drawers banged on the left while the fridge door flew open and sprayed its contents onto the moving floor. We were awash in food, dishes, and broken glass, while pictures were ripped off the walls and bookshelves crashed to the floor.

I had my eyes fixed on my mum who was holding onto an ironing board. It was a miracle she didn't surf off through one of the windows. I was holding onto the somewhat more secure kitchen bench.

After what seemed like an eternity the shaking and noise finally came to a sudden stop . . . silence.

"Let's get out of here," I yelled to my mum. We sprinted downstairs, jumped over fallen chairs, books, broken flower pots and a huge heavy heater that had been ripped off the wall. We made it outside just before the next violent shock rocked the ground.

Once we were outside the house, in the relative safety of the open air, I looked toward town. Beautiful Christchurch was anything but picturesque now. A huge dust cloud hung over the city, black smoke billowed from the city center and one of the tall buildings was clearly leaning to one side. I knew then that this was an earthquake beyond any previous shakes Christchurch had experienced. Although only 6.3 on the Richter scale, the epicenter had been right under the city and the results were unimaginable! One-hundred eighty-five people were killed, homes destroyed, businesses ruined, roads made impassable, and 20-30 billion in NZ dollar damage. Christchurch was truly 'munted' (New Zealand word for destroyed).

Sirens started whaling and didn't stop for a long time. It was about 45 minutes before I could confirm by text that my son and some other friends were okay. For days we were without running water, there was no electricity, no telephone, no Internet. Several people I texted never replied. Sadly they were amongst those who had lost their lives that day—eleven of those were my friends and work colleagues.

After a while we realized how 'lucky' we had been—if that's even the right word. I had canceled a client earlier in the morning, because I wasn't feeling a hundred percent. Not canceling this client would have put us in my 1st floor clinic where we surely would have been injured if not killed. The clinic, which had been a gorgeous, wooden historic building, received a red sticker. This meant it was deemed too unsafe to even enter and had to be demolished. Everything was lost including much of my office equipment. Not canceling that client would have put my mum right into the city center, maybe even on the 14th floor of that high-rise building. I shudder to think how circumstances could have been so different if not for one single change of plans.

Instead, we were in one of the most solid houses on the hill. We were together when I confirmed that my son was okay as well as many friends. We had water, food and even a bottle of bubbly. We felt so protected and looked after, and filled with incredible gratitude. It felt like a miracle.

Fast forward three weeks—my mum left Christchurch as soon as she could after the quake, along with thousands of other people. The reality of the disaster and the unbelievable level of destruction and devastation were life-changing. Christchurch was like a war zone. The military used tanks to cordon off the inner city. Every day was a matter of survival. People walked around like zombies on autopilot. Three or four times every night aftershocks woke us all up with a start. We were ready to bolt for the door at the slightest vibration. Adrenalin always seemed on the edge of pumping, so anxiety levels ran high.

Along with many of my belongings, I had also lost many of my commitments: rental and lease agreements, phone and Internet contracts, all dissolved in the devastation of the earthquake. I found myself free—traumatized yes—but free!

What now? What was I going to do? I needed to get out of Christchurch. Many wild thoughts coursed through my agitated brain. Should I move to the north island and start a new business or should I travel? Traveling sounded better!

I decided to leave my business, my sons, my friends and the place

I had called home for twenty years. But where to go?

Do I have the confidence? Will I be able to make enough money to live? Will the next place be any safer than here? Am I crazy for leaving behind everything I had created?

Following the earthquake, I had been struggling with sadness, grief and the sense of loss. Now fear, doubt and confusion felt like they would consume me.

Fear of the unknown was paralyzing me. I realized that I was projecting disempowering thoughts into my future, creating scenarios that really might not ever happen. As soon as I became aware of what I was doing to myself, I began to change my thinking with empowering affirmations.

Yes, I am facing the unknown, but this means limitless possibilities. It means adventure. It means meeting amazing people and having life-enriching experiences. It means living my dream. I have always wanted to travel, combining work and leisure. The next step of my adventure became clear. I would live life to the max! I would go to Los Angeles!

I arrived in Los Angeles on April 1, 2011. It was fantastic being met by a longtime dear friend and her precious puppy. She took me to all my favorite places in L.A., like Lake Shrine, where I had an opportunity to physically and spiritually recharge. But I still felt out of control, insecure, lost. As soon as I became aware and began to let go, I realized that I had a fantastic opportunity to learn to be truly present in the *Now*. Cultivating trust and faith, I felt my angst melt away like butter in the hot L.A. sun.

The friend I was staying with highly recommended a remarkable healer near Sedona. So I made an appointment with the fellow, picked up a rental car, and was off the next day for Arizona! A road trip—Yay!

I had a blast cruising along. At first it took all my attention to drive on the 'wrong' side of the road. (In New Zealand, we drive on the opposite side.) When I was able to relax more, I marveled at my journey, enjoying the vastness of the landscape. I was thrilled to see the first saguaro cactus! Arizona, here we are!

I had no idea where all this would lead me, but I was okay with it. The adventure had truly begun. In Phoenix, I decided to take time to reconnect with that place of stillness and centeredness within myself, a place I had temporarily lost during the trauma and upheaval of the prior few weeks. If my money ran out within the next few weeks, so be it. I would just continue my trip to Germany, where I could easily find work.

As soon as I decided to relax and let go, amazing things started to happen. I didn't know anybody in Sedona, so I put out a request to the Universe to help me find a place to stay for a while. The following day, after meditation, I started to chat with a lady. She told me that she had a friend from Sedona staying with her at the moment and introduced me to her. Within two minutes I had an invitation to stay in Sedona for the week.

In addition, a friend gave me the contact information for a guy with whom I might be able to stay with in Phoenix. I noticed a little smile on her face. I had an urge to ask whether he was single, but held back. I didn't want to seem too keen to meet a man.

So after a couple of days in Phoenix, I decided to give Kevin a call. We arranged to meet up after the Sunday service at our church. When I asked him how I was going to recognize him, he answered in his deep voice with a hint of flirtatiousness, "Well, let me see . . . tall, dark, handsome, intelligent, accomplished—" which was followed by his inimitable, infectious laugh. I was even more curious to meet this man!

At church, I took one of two empty seats in the middle of a row. Just before the service began, a handsome man sat down next to me. Of course, I wasn't looking too closely, because after all I was there for God.

After the service, the gentleman disappeared and I made my way out of the church, chatting here and there with friendly looking devotees, heading to the arranged meeting place. I couldn't help feeling some butterflies in my stomach.

I was very surprised to find that the same man who had sat beside me in church was Kevin! Out of a congregation of over two-hundred, he had chosen the seat right next to me! Kevin casually remarked that he figured I was the German Kiwi (*Kiwi* is colloquial for New Zealander).

After a lovely lunch with Kevin and one of his friends, it was time to part. Kevin piped up, "Would you like to come see my acrobatic trapeze?"

Well, how could I refuse an invitation like that? I followed him back to his lovely home. To say we hit it off would be an understatement. We had a fantastic afternoon playing like kids on the trapeze (who has a 24-foot high trapeze in their backyard?), the slack line, the trampoline, and ended up throwing each other in the pool. I had hardly ever felt so much at ease with a guy and had so much fun! But we had only just met, so we were both cautious not to give too much away. Wow, what an unexpected and amazing encounter!

I ended up finding reasons to extend my stay week by week, enjoying Sedona and its breathtaking rock formations and awe-inspiring views. The ancientness of Sedona felt strangely familiar—the perfect location to heal my frayed nerves and stressed body.

I spent my weekends with Kevin and attending the many wonderful meditations and services at the Self-Realization Fellowship Church in Phoenix. As we got better acquainted, I helped him with some of his projects, where we discovered what a great team we made. We meditated together, and went jet skiing, and dancing (he's a swing dancer!) We got along like a house on fire.

Finally my three-month visitor visa came to an end, as well as my finances. I had to say goodbye to my new friends, to beautiful Sedona and saddest of all to Kevin, not knowing whether or when I would see any of them again. My heart felt like it was breaking. Arizona had started to feel like home, my new friends had started to feel like family, and with Kevin I sensed a potential upon which we had only touched. I guess both of us had been hurt before and felt somewhat guarded, and maybe the logistics of living in opposite parts of the world seemed daunting.

Off I went to Munich, Germany, my old hometown, again not knowing what the future would hold. I had a great summer and I enjoyed catching up with family and friends from the past. However, I was pining for Kevin. Wasn't he getting it that there was something special between us? I was determined not to chase him, but why wasn't he keeping in touch? If somebody had asked me how I imagined the perfect man, I would have described Kevin. I adored everything about him. I loved his playfulness, spontaneity, creativity, and wisdom. He was the embodiment of youth, energy and vitality, and although I realize that I may have been a bit lovesick, I thought he looked like a Greek god!

But why wasn't he interested in me? Sadly, I just had to put him out of my mind and let him go. So I got involved with life in Munich, found some work, went to dance classes, and eventually even put my profile on several Internet dating sites.

And then it finally happened. Kevin called me on my mobile! He was missing me and was keen to explore the possibility of a relationship. He also had gone to an astrologer (a Sedona astrologer!) to have a compatibility report prepared, which convinced him to give us a shot. After I had been in Germany for four months, Kevin invited me to come and visit him again. I literally jumped on the next plane. I couldn't wait to feel his strong arms around me. What a joyful reunion! Four months apart had only made our attraction and budding love for each other stronger.

Meanwhile, Kevin had been to Sedona many times looking at houses for sale. He had lived in the city long enough and felt he needed a change. He was looking forward to showing me the new home he had purchased. I was equally excited. And what a magnificent home and property it was: high ceilings, spacious, sunny, with a great deck from which to enjoy gorgeous views of Capitol Butte and Chimney Rock. And the most touching thing, he carried me across the threshold!

POSTSCRIPT: I'm now living the dream with Kevin, the love of my life, in a loving home and magnificent environment. My heart can hardly contain the gratitude and joy. I feel like I'm living in the palm of God's hand. What an incredible journey it has been, from trauma and devastation, to love and beauty. This journey has given new meaning to the expression, 'When one door closes another opens!'

CHAPTER FIFTEEN
Through the Fire

Rose Davis is a Registered Nurse with forty years' experience and works at Verde Valley Medical Center. She's written several nursing articles for professional journals about grief, death, patient advocacy, and she's a contributing author to *Touched by a Nurse* (Lippincott Williams & Wilkins, 1999). Rose is 60 and has lived in Sedona for two years.

Bryan Davis holds a M.A from Adelphi University and has been a teacher at Patchogue-Medford Public School for thirty-one years in Medford, NY. He spent two years with the NYPD; is a Viet Nam veteran and retired from the U.S. Marine Corps. Bryan is 61 and has lived in Sedona for two years.

My name is Rose. I'm writing this memoir. After the death of my husband Mickey, and after the death of Bryan's wife Eva, we each separately wandered around in a fog. Neither of us knew the other yet. Bryan was in New York, I was in Sedona. Grief rolled around inside us and raised its head constantly. You see couples walking around together and you want to scream, "I lost my spouse! I hurt! I ache!" You hear music and it makes you sob. Your grief is always so near the surface. But before I go on, I must go back and tell our story as it unfolded.

2006—Mickey and Rose

Mickey and I lived in Kansas City. We had visited Sedona for years and like so many, it captured our hearts. We bought a condo in 1995 to gain a toe hold in Sedona in anticipation of moving there and eventually building a home. In 1998, we bought an acre of land in the Village and felt we were realizing our dream. In 2006, we decided to move to Sedona. As a nurse, I was easily able to find work at Flagstaff Medical Center. So in May 2006, we packed the car with our dog, our parrot and belongings, and set out for Sedona. The movers would bring the rest of our things, furniture and our second car. It was a long drive with one overnight, but we arrived safely.

2006—Bryan and Eva

They were living on Long Island, New York. They were both teachers. Bryan retired in 2004 while Eva continued to work. They had also been to Sedona many times and dreamed of building their dream home. They had bought and sold a few parcels of land until they found the perfect spot to build and plans were set in motion—architect selected, builder secured and the construction began. Eva and Bryan planned exactly what they wanted in their home—a pool, hot tub, 60-inch dining room table, and a three-car garage big enough for Bryan's passion of classic muscle cars. Several trips were made to Sedona and emails went back and forth to oversee the building of their dream home. Ground was broken in the winter of 2007.

Mickey and Rose

In the meantime, my husband Mickey was so enamored with Sedona. He and I would sit at Starbucks and look over the red rocks. We couldn't believe we lived in this beautiful, peaceful place. Mickey was retired, but wanted something to do during the day so he went to work for the Chamber of Commerce. He had the 'gift of gab' and loved talking to visitors telling them about the area, the fun things to do and where to eat. I commuted to Flagstaff Medical Center and drove up the canyon road several days during the week. We settled in our condo and got used to our routine. In early 2007, I suggested we start looking for a contractor to start planning our dream home. Mickey was several years older than me and didn't want to build a home when he was in his 70s. We started having discussions and asking friends who they would recommend. Finally, we were ready with our plans of how we wanted the home laid out, what kind of fixtures we wanted, and what kind of décor. We had saved volumes of pictures for years and we knew exactly what we wanted. The future we dreamed of was finally taking shape.

Bryan and Eva

Eva always had a nagging ear blockage. In 1988, six months after Bryan and Eva were married, she was diagnosed with a tumor in her sinus area. Surgeons removed the tumor and said she was fine; they had gotten all of the tumor out. She had forty-five radiation treatments, and they were told they would continue to do MRI's to make sure everything was all right.

In 1996, during one of Eva's routine MRI's, the radiologist found the tumor had returned. They returned to Denver where the specialist was and she had surgery again. After a long surgery they told Eva and Bryan that they got the entire tumor again and the margins were clear. She had another 45 rounds of radiation. She continued to work as a reading teacher while she had her radiation treatments and she improved steadily.

Mickey and Rose

In June 2007, Mickey noticed an uncomfortable feeling in his lower belly area. He had a history of kidney stones and felt it was probably a stone causing his discomfort. He made an appointment with his urologist and the doctor told him he was simply having bladder infections. However, he started having fevers and sweats throughout the summer and was on and off antibiotics. He felt a little run down, but attributed it to walking the dog frequently. He had lost some weight which was good because he was a little heavy. One day in early September, he was in front of the mirror in the bathroom when I was shocked to see his ribs sticking out. I knew something was very wrong.

Bryan and Eva

Nine years had passed for Bryan and Eva and after many MRI's and CAT scans everything came back negative until June, 2007. The surgeon in Denver reviewing the scans noticed a subtle change. He corresponded with the surgeon at NYU medical center. Eva needed to have some teeth removed and while they were in that area they biopsied the area that looked suspicious. The biopsy came back cancerous once again. After receiving the heartbreaking news they began to prepare for another big surgery to once again remove the cancerous tumor.

Eva was in the hospital for three weeks ultimately coming home with a feeding tube and dressing changes on her leg from where the skin graft was taken. The graft was to help close and heal the surgically repaired area in her mouth. The wound on her leg was so large, and always trying to find humor in every situation, they decided they would tell everyone "she was bitten by a shark."

About a week after Eva came home from the hospital, the feeding tube became dislodged while she was sleeping and she was unable get the liquid food into her stomach. They went to the emergency room to have it reinserted. The surgeon was unable to reinsert the tube and she was sent to NYU Medical Center where she stayed another two weeks, where they put the tube back in without anesthesia. She had become very weak and had lost a lot of weight. They went back home again.

While she was at home she enjoyed watching comedy shows like *I Love Lucy* which would bring her laughter. While on the couch which was also her bed she'd ring a bell when she wanted Bryan to put the nutritional solution in her feeding tube.

It was a Sunday evening. Eva was on the couch watching her shows while Bryan was upstairs watching a ballgame. At 10:00 p.m. she didn't ring the bell, but Bryan thought she had just fallen asleep which often happened. By 11:00 p.m. since she hadn't rung the bell, Bryan went downstairs to check on her and found her unresponsive. He called 911, then immediately started CPR. The ambulance took her to the hospital, but efforts at resuscitation failed. Eva had battled cancer for 21 years and succumbed to it on July 29th.

Mickey and Rose

I asked the urologist to do a biopsy on Mickey because I had a bad feeling. On October 2, 2007, the biopsy was done. It came back malignant. The surgeon said we needed to have his bladder removed as soon as possible because the tumor was already golf ball size. We went into high gear talking to Mickey's best friend in Kansas City who was a surgeon with a contact at Mayo Clinic. We set up appointments and started Internet searches so we'd know what to expect with the surgery. We made several trips to Rochester, Minnesota to the Mayo Clinic for doctors' appointments, then headed back to Sedona.

Mickey started getting very weak and had no appetite. He was in the hospital in Cottonwood, then back to the Mayo Clinic. They wanted to start chemotherapy, but he had fevers and abnormal blood work, so they wanted to wait until his fevers stopped and his blood work improved. Meanwhile, he grew even weaker. He couldn't even climb the stairs to go to bed. He started falling when he got up to go to the bathroom. I couldn't leave him alone. I became so frightened I was beside myself while I helplessly watched his decline. He was fading away. The tumor had grown so large so rapidly that it burst through his bladder into his colon. On Friday evening a surgeon was brought in to take him to emergency surgery to repair the hole.

After surgery he was on a breathing machine and in ICU at Verde Valley Medical Center in Cottonwood. I knew the outlook was bleak and wanted desperately to get him back to his family in Kansas City. I flew him back by air ambulance on Wednesday. He was admitted to the ICU where his best friend was a surgeon. Mickey's daughter, his son and other family members and friends gathered to offer prayers and support.

On Saturday morning the doctor caring for him asked to privately see me and his children. He told us the cancer had spread all over his body and now had spread to his brain. He said Mickey would never be able to be taken off the breathing machine. He told us there was nothing more anyone could do for him and asked if we wanted to keep him on life support. I knew Mickey would not want to be kept alive on a machine—we had talked about that in the past and he'd written it into his Living Will. Mickey's children and I discussed it and painfully decided to take him off the respirator. All the family and his friends kept a vigil in the waiting room. I sat at his bedside with his children in the room as we waited for the inevitable. Six agonizing hours later he stopped breathing.

New Beginnings

Mickey died December 15, 2007, six months before Eva died, and Eva's death occurred only two weeks before completion of her and Bryan's new home. Coincidentally, Mickey and Eva never saw their dream houses.

After Mickey passed, I stayed in Sedona for eight months, then I had to get out. I would come home from work and think I saw him sitting in his chair. I would go to places we went and could only feel the heavy ache of grief and loneliness. I moved back to Kansas City, went back to my old job at the hospital and moved into an apartment across the street from my step-daughter. I felt if I could be around family and friends it might make the sadness go away.

In the meantime, Bryan was living on Long Island. His house in Sedona was completed but empty. Why come live by yourself in Sedona? All his friends were in New York. What would he do by himself in Sedona?

Two years went by and the loan on his Sedona house was coming due. Being in grief fog and not knowing what else to do, he decided to move to Sedona, put the newly completed house up for sale and search for what would bring him happiness. He figured he could be just as lonely in Sedona as he was in New York. He sold his home on Long Island and one week before Christmas in 2009, he put his Golden Retriever Mac in the U-Haul and with that best friend made the long drive to Sedona.

While in Kansas City, I was experiencing deep feelings of sadness, loneliness and emptiness. I still had property and a condo in Sedona, but was hesitating to go back there to take care of my financial responsibilities, but I knew I had to start to search for what would bring *me* happiness. I had two mortgages and a rent payment—that didn't make a lot of financial sense. My old job at the hospital in Cottonwood had become available, and that finally motivated me to make the move back to Sedona. On Memorial weekend 2010, I packed my car, my parrot and some belongings and headed out.

June 2010, I was sitting outside the New York Bagel shop near my condo with my dog. The owner of the shop, Ross, came out to talk with me.

"Hi Rose, I wanted to let you know that Bryan's back in town," he said.

I must have looked befuddled. "Bryan—Bryan who? I don't know anyone named Bryan," I said.

Now Ross was looking a bit befuddled. He went inside the shop and brought Bryan out to meet me. I didn't know it at the time, but Bryan had told Ross he didn't want to meet anyone. He just wanted to eat his bagel and drink his coffee and be left alone. Ross was persistent and brought Bryan outside to meet me. We shook hands and Bryan said he felt an immediate spark with me. I was oblivious! I didn't feel a thing!

I usually went to the bagel shop on weekends. I would walk my dog there, sit outside, read the paper and visit with tourists. As time progressed and I would periodically see Bryan. He felt more comfortable coming over and talking with me. It was so comforting to share experiences with someone who had been through the fire. People don't always understand grief unless they've been through it. We talked many times over the summer months and through our talking got to know each other. The talks were helping us both to continue working through our grief.

In trying to figure out his life, Bryan had gone back to Long Island several times over the summer. He finally decided over Labor Day weekend that he was going back to New York to live. He told me one Saturday morning that he would sell his house and get on with his life back in New York. I told him he needed to do what would be best for him. Walking home that morning I felt a huge sadness. My friend was leaving. I knew I would probably be moving somewhere else in the next two years myself so I didn't blame him for leaving. We needed to get on with our lives and find some direction. It's hard to decide what your plans are for the future when you had those plans all figured out, but the plans get shattered with the death of your spouse. You just feel you're floating around in life without much direction.

Well, as it turned out, Bryan's home wasn't selling because the market was so depressed. Meanwhile, he and I started to go to the movies and dinner. We started looking at each other differently and realized we had a nice connection. We wanted to spend more time together and we did. We officially became a couple in October, got engaged in January and were married in July, 2012.

POSTCRIPT: We often talk of the Sedona magic. Why did we both feel compelled to move back to Sedona? We were two separate souls with separate lives, yet we both came cross country to return to Sedona. I feel we were destined to meet. Some say Eva and Mickey brought us together. We don't know. We just know that there can be extraordinary happiness after tragedy and there can be unexpected new beginnings later in life. We are proof of that, right here in Sedona.

CHAPTER SIXTEEN
Flying High

Karen Lombardi is a dental technician/dental laboratory owner. She loves to hike, play bingo, and build and fly airplanes with her husband Tom. Nine years ago she and Tom moved to Sedona from Southern California, where she grew up. Karen is 50 years old.

One wonders how things happen in life and why? Some people including myself are a believer that things happen for a reason. You deal with it the best you can and move on. Little did I know that our lives and the lives of six other people would change by following a feeling and taking a leap of faith.

Back in the late 1990s, we had visited Sedona in our motorhome for a weekend. We were awestruck by its sheer splendor. We lived in Southern California where we owned a home and had our own business with a few employees. We were basically weekend travelers and led very busy lives. We were involved in an ultralight aircraft club that did weekend get-togethers with motorhomes and airplanes. In the early 2000s, the club did a couple of fly-ins to Sedona. We stayed at a hotel on top of the airport mesa. We would stand at the airport lookout and just gaze at the landscape. There was truly something magical about the area. I am not a deeply religious person nor am I a believer in magical healing crystals and what not, but I felt a certain calming and something that truly touched my soul when I was there.

Back at home the following year we were told there was a neighborhood meeting regarding future development behind our housing track. I went to find out what this was about. We had lived in our home for seventeen years—a beautiful lot up on a hill. Below us was a valley with a commercial nursery and a mountain range. It was a great view. The meeting was called by a developer who had plans to build 350 homes right behind us, and we were one of the most affected. We thought to ourselves maybe it's time to get out of Southern California! Business had been great, we were happy, it all seemed so wrong to leave. Then we planned a weekend trip—Sedona here we come!

A couple we knew from the airport club heard we were driving to Sedona for the weekend and wanted to follow us there. We told them we had business to do first. We wanted to talk with prospective clients in the field of our business to see if it would be viable to continue it in Sedona, and we had a day set up with a real estate broker to look at houses. What were we doing?

We arrived on a Friday in May, 2004. We kind of canvassed different offices to talk with would-be future clients for our business. Happy to find out there was a need for our dental services and they were excited at the possibility of us coming to town, we went up to the airport to take a break before meeting with the real estate agent. On a prior visit to Sedona we had met a guy who was building the same kit airplane. We stopped by his hangar to see his progress, but the hangar doors were open and the plane was gone. My husband was excited and said he must have finished it and was out flying! When he returned from his flight and showed us the plane, (he remembered us from before) we all decided to go to breakfast at the airport restaurant. My husband was very concerned about storing our plane at the Sedona airport. We had talked with many people about how difficult it was to find a hangar to rent or buy.

In the middle of breakfast this guy walks over to our friend and asks him if he knows anyone who wants to rent a hangar! My husband raised his hand. He was a bit freaked out by the coincidence. I expressed that we hadn't even looked at houses yet and he wants to rent a hangar? He said we had to grab this quickly and sign a six-month lease that morning if we wanted it. I felt a bit strange to say the least at what was happening.

Were the stars aligning or just pure coincidence?

We had sent a list of our desires to the agent in advance so she realized our needs. The first house we looked at had so many things on our list it was creepy! The view out the front of the house was amazing, right below Capital Butte or as the locals call it, Thunder Mountain. We spent the next several hours looking at homes and nothing compared to the first one. We went back a second time and put an offer on the house. I was so confused yet so excited! We hadn't even listed our home for sale yet, this was too much, what was happening? We went home and put our house up for sale. It sold in ten days! We packed and closed our business and were in Sedona thirty days later! A leap of faith or just meant to be?

In the following few years, friends of ours from our ultralight club decided to sell their homes and pack up. All in all, three couples from our club all left their homes and jobs in Southern California and followed us out here. Their lives all changed because of what we did.

Before we left California I had lost my dad and one of my sisters to heart disease. She was in her early forties, too much stress, overweight and no time to deal with her health. It was devastating to me. After moving here I lost one of my brothers and my mom to the same horrible disease. In California, I and other family members were on high blood pressure medicine, cholesterol medicine and struggled with being overweight. Moving to Sedona made me realize how precious life is every day. I started hiking and walking. I joined Weight Watchers and lost over forty pounds. I'm now off all medicines except one. I still wake up every day and see the beauty all around me. I just celebrated my 50th birthday earlier this year. I don't feel fifty!

I hike our beautiful trails and run into people visiting all the time. They ask where I'm from and I proudly say that I live here. They're amazed and wish they could too. I tell them I used to say the same thing when I came to visit. So many things happened, and too many things lined up when we were trying to figure out if this was the thing we were supposed to do. Our lives have changed in every aspect for the good. I look forward to growing old with my husband and sharing the rest of our lives in this beautiful and amazing place. Can a place call to you? Yes. Is there something magical about this place? Yes. I love Sedona.

Bell Rock with Century Plants - ©Jim Peterson

Thunder Mountain from Turkey Creek - ©Jim Peterson

Courthouse Butte - ©Jim Peterson

Boynton Canyon, East Wall - ©Jim Peterson

Chimney Rock from Jim Thompson Trail - ©Jim Peterson

Snoopy Rock from Marg's Draw Trail - ©Jim Peterson

Kachina Woman after Winter Storm - ©Jim Peterson

Monsoon Sunset at Cathedral Rock - ©Jim Peterson

The Cow Pies - ©Jim Peterson

Devil's Bridge - ©Jim Peterson

The Seven Warriors - ©Jim Peterson

Coffee Pot Rock in Winter - ©Jim Peterson

Jim Peterson is a professional photographer living in Sedona. His passion for rich, superbly detailed images of the natural world is articulated through a singular blend of classic photographic methods and state-of-the-art digital techniques. His body of work ranges from small, intimate portraits of wild beings to majestic, room-sized landscapes and panoramas. He accepts assignments for architectural, fine art reproduction, and portrait photography. Jim can be reached at (928)554-4340. Many more of his images can be seen at www.JamesPeterson.name.

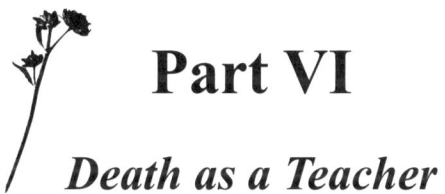

Part VI
Death as a Teacher

"There are two ways to live life. One is as though nothing is a miracle, the other is as though everything is a miracle."

—Albert Einstein [in Dellinger DT (1993), *From Yale to Jail: The Life Story of a Moral Dissenter:* 418.]

CHAPTER SEVENTEEN
The Healer

 **Shawn Bieber** is a sixth grade teacher at Oak Creek School in Cornville where she shares her love of writing with her students. She and her husband Mike live in Sedona where they spend their free time hiking the majestic red rock mountains. Shawn is 45 and has lived in Sedona about a year.

I think back as I write this—overlooking Oak Creek Canyon and it's splendor—to the first time just a few short years ago of my arrival here. I was not conscious of its beauty and the magic it would have in store as my new husband and I were driving along Highway 179 from Sky Harbor Airport, Phoenix, to begin our seven-day honeymoon.

It took me forty years to find Mike, the man I would fall madly in love with. This man was my best friend, confidant, co-worker, lover, and soon to be husband. We had been toying with ideas of where to honeymoon. We were not the conventional type. My wedding ensemble consisted of a long, vibrant red dress and Harley Davidson motorcycle boots. We wed atop a wooden bridge on a trail with very few family members and the icy sleet gray skies of Indiana on April 12, 2008. Though it was cold and dismal outside, we were giddy with laughter and permanent smiles.

Prior to that blissful day, we had wondered where we should honeymoon. Would it be on the white beaches of Jamaica or in a secluded cabin in the Appalachian Mountains? My mother, who had always wanted to visit Sedona, suggested that we go to the place she had heard that had vortexes, crystals, and miraculous ways of healing. She herself was a healer of sorts, a dedicated social worker. She cleansed her chakras with every crystal imaginable and talked to the angels around her. She wanted Mike and me to experience what she had always wanted to, but unfortunately never had the opportunity. She had already battled her first bout of a rare type of brain cancer for adults—medulloblastoma. At the age of 57, she had been dealing with dizzy spells and debilitating headaches. She had visited several doctors and had a MRI on her brain. No one, not even the radiologist could detect anything.

The symptoms progressed and she finally sought out one of the top neurologists in the country. She was fortunate to get in to see him, and as luck would have it, he was my father's friend and co-worker. Though divorced, she and my father separated on speaking terms. My father was a surgical assistant, and Dr. John would only operate with him by his side. My mother was grateful to have been seen by him. It took only one glance at her films for him to see the almost undetectable tumor. He knew right away prognosis would not be good. By the time he and my father delicately extracted the tumor, it had grown to nine centimeters—the size of a large lemon. They were unable to get a few of the 'fingers' of the tumor, but with almost deadly radiation, her survival rate would be 60%.

The next few months brought radiation to her delicate body that was so intense she was deemed a guinea pig. Since the cancer was normally detected in children, the radiologist had to give her the highest level of radiation to her head and spine to hopefully kill the cancerous cells that Dr. John could not surgically remove. As is so often typical, the radiation alone almost killed her as she battled side effects. She was a warrior during these months of agony. My sister and I would give her support, love, and push her to her limits to find her internal strength to go to one more radiation therapy session. We would wipe the tears, clean up the vomit, and find her underneath her bed banging on the wall for help—lost, scared and confused. The radiation literally fried her brain, but fortunately gave her back 80% of the life she was used to, although she was never quite the same. Mike had only met my mother briefly before the cancer occurred. He never got to hear her rich sense of humor, laughter or see the true brightness in her eyes.

She loved Mike. She was so excited for us to honeymoon in Sedona, and tell her all about our adventures of vortexes, hikes into past history and crystal magic. On our first vortex hike to Mystic Vista, a pain that I had for over a year in my foot was gone the next morning! I knew then that I wanted to bring my mom here to be healed of her cancer! On the third day of our enchanted honeymoon, my sister had regretfully told me that our mom had lost her balance (a side effect of the radiation) and broke her hip! What more could our dear mother endure? I wanted to gather her in my arms and lay her down on top of a miraculous vortex to take away her pains as it had done for me.

We knew after our first visit to Sedona that we would move here in six years with our blended family, enough time for our youngest daughter to graduate high school and get the oldest through college. Within those years, my mom's cancer had come back. Mike and I never had the chance to bring her to our beloved Sedona. She didn't have the luxury of having Dr. John and my father perform the surgery. My father passed away from lung cancer. Though she had a second craniotomy, mom was given only six months to live. Radiation was not an option. She was not scared to die. She accepted her short time left and lived and loved to the fullest. We lost our beloved mother on February 27, 2009. She was only 62.

As Mike and I hiked to the top of Mystic Vista on our next visit, I shouted "Hi Mom!" I felt her come through me saying she had finally made it here. I had buried her mala beads at the top of Mystic Vista underneath a swirling tree. We knew our move was closer than expected. We went back to Indiana, sold everything we had, packed our bags, headed west, and have been living in the splendor of Sedona since. We took our daughters on an evening hike to Mystic Vista the other day, and as I reached the top, I shouted to my mom again. The wind blew as she told me she was still here . . . on the wing of the red rock mountains and crystal blue skies.

CHAPTER EIGHTEEN
Free Fall

Kristen M. Huard is the very proud mother of 1 year-old daughter Anya Jade. The two of them love to travel. Kristen is currently finishing a book she hopes will motivate and inspire others to live life to the fullest. She's 31 and lived in Sedona for seven years prior to her more recent residency of four years. [www.TheEndlessHorizon.com]

I first moved to Sedona in 1992. I was twelve years old and like any kid my age I was quite apprehensive about starting a new school. Sedona was quite different than Chico, California from where we came. It was very different going from such a big school to such a little school. However, I adjusted well and made new friends. I liked living in Sedona.

As the years went on I became interested in hiking and exploring the outdoors. I fell in love with the beauty of Sedona and soaked in the deep red of the rocks. It seemed to feed my soul. I couldn't spend enough time outside on trails. My mom was a massage therapist. One of her clients was a local dentist. During one of his massages he told my mom that he was looking for a high school student to work in his office part time. My mom instantly thought about me and before I knew it I was working in a dental office. I loved it! I learned a lot about dentistry and about running an office.

I graduated from high school and moved to Los Angeles. My older brother, Dustin had moved out there the prior year. My brother and I were very close. Growing up with a single mom we were very thankful to have each other. We became best friends. My brother loved me the way every child should love their sibling. I feel very blessed for that. It was Dustin who introduced me to the red rocks of Sedona. We would go hiking together every single day before he moved to California. Dustin and I got an apartment together on the beach in Santa Monica. It was a strange adjustment. The beauty of the ocean felt familiar while it took a while to get used to all of the people.

Dustin and I lived together in Los Angeles for eight years. In 1996, I decided that I wanted to try something new, I would go skydiving! I found a place in Southern California and made my first skydive—Perris Valley Skydiving. I loved it! I decided at that moment this was a challenge that I wanted to take on. I wanted to compete. I wanted to teach others and I wanted to travel. Looking back at this dream helped me come to terms with the phrase, *Be careful what you wish for!*

Within the year I had 500 skydives. I was a United States Parachute Association certified coach teaching students how to skydive. I was an aerial photographer shooting photos and videos of skydivers. I was the winner of a bronze medal from the US Nationals in 8-way formation skydiving. Lastly, I had purchased my airline tickets to begin my around-the-world trip.

I left in January 2007 and returned to the states in December. I had an amazing time traveling and skydiving, seeing the world from above. I learned a lot about myself, about life and about what is truly important to me. Returning to Los Angeles after spending time in places like India and Africa was one of the hardest things I have ever done. To go from where they have nothing, but are thankful for the gift of life, to where people have everything yet feel it's not enough, was difficult. I didn't last long in L.A. I yearned for a sense of humility among others and a true sense of community. I wanted to be surrounded by people who valued life and the beauty of nature. I told Dustin how hard it was for me to be in Los Angeles. We talked about it a lot since he could see my struggle.

After being in L.A. for 6 months I received a call from my former employer. In July 2008, the dentist I worked for in Sedona offered me a job! He called me asking me if I wanted to move back to Sedona and run his office. He offered to compensate me well in addition to providing me with excellent benefits. He also offered to move me back to Sedona from Los Angeles. I hung up the phone and was so excited. I called Dustin right away and told him the exciting news and that I was probably going to move back to Sedona. He was very happy for me.

After some thought Dustin decided he would also move back to Sedona. He was over Los Angeles and ready for a positive change, just like me. Our plan was to pack up a U-Haul and get a place together in Sedona. We would continue to be roommates. I told the dentist in Sedona what the plan was and he was ecstatic. A few hours later he called me back. He said he had a patient who just came in to the office who has a home for rent with the option to buy. He sent me photos and got me in touch with the patient. Before we knew it we had a nice, new three-bedroom home. Our plan was to rent together with the hope of buying it. Things were working out nicely!

On August 1, 2008, we left Los Angeles. Dustin was driving the U-Haul and I was following him in my car. Dustin left his car in L.A., because he had to come back to finish a job. He worked as a production assistant in Hollywood. He worked on numerous commercials and music videos. Dustin was an independent contractor so he could be selective in his choice of jobs. He had previously committed to working on a commercial mid-August so he would go back to L.A. and stay with our cousin for three days while he finished work. Our cousin was out of the country so this worked out well. Dustin's plan was to return back to Sedona at the end of August to get unpacked and settled in.

I started work at the dental office on August 15th. I was so happy to be getting settled in and really enjoying my new life in Sedona. I had a newfound appreciation for the community, my employer, my family and the beauty of the red rocks. I was flying high on cloud nine without even jumping out of an airplane! I decided to check out Red Rock Skydiving in

Cottonwood. I brought my skydiving equipment as well as all of my video equipment. Once I got out there I introduced myself to everyone. The owner saw my video equipment and asked if I was interested in working there as a videographer. What are the chances? I was prepared to pay to skydive and suddenly had the opportunity to get paid to skydive!

This was a dream! I accepted the job and began to skydive every weekend shooting photos and videos of tandem passengers who were going skydiving for the first time. In my eyes, life didn't get much better than this! I kept telling Dustin that I was going to take him skydiving. We were making plans for his tandem skydive when he returned home. I would jump with him and shoot his video. We were both really looking forward to that.

Dustin had been in L.A. for about two weeks. I received a call from him on my way home from work on a Wednesday afternoon. He had just been in a terrible car accident. He was working, doing a run for the producer to get ice from the gas station. He was stopped at a red light and someone ran the red light. The guy who ran the red light crashed into someone else who was turning left at the intersection.

The two cars then collided and slid into the car my brother was driving. Because the accident happened while he was working, everything needed to be taken care of by worker comp. Dustin went to the emergency room and was released that evening. He was told that he had severe trauma to his left knee. Dustin went back to my cousin's house with a knee brace and crutches. He had an MRI and it was determined that he needed surgery.

I was very concerned about Dustin. He didn't have anyone to help him while my cousin was out of town, so my mom and I decided to go to L.A. to help him. I told him that we wanted to come out and bring him back to Sedona. He really wanted to do that, but was informed that if he left the state of California he would be financially responsible for all of the medical bills from the accident up until that point. Dustin felt trapped. He could not afford to pay those bills. He felt like he didn't have a choice but to stay in

Los Angeles and have his knee surgery, so he was waiting for workers comp to approve the surgery. From what he told me the whole system was making him jump through hoops to get approval. My poor brother was in so much pain. He was under the care of two physicians who were contracted workers comp doctors. They had him on a ton of pain medication as well as muscle relaxants until the surgery was approved.

Three weeks went by and he was not doing well. On Thursday, October 1, 2008, I was trying to call him all day. I was really worried. Something inside just didn't feel right. He didn't sound like himself when I would speak with him on the phone. I was talking to my mom about it and she felt the same way. That day we made a plan to drive out to Los Angeles. We didn't care what workers comp said. Our plan was to go get Dustin and bring him back to Sedona. The most important thing was that Dustin be home with family where we could care for him.

That evening we received a very disturbing phone call. My brother, my best friend, passed away in his sleep the evening prior. A friend of his found him. This was the hardest thing my family has ever endured. There were so many unanswered questions and feelings of helplessness. It was too late. We were told that my brother died from taking the medication. I truly believe that workers comp was responsible for the loss of my brother. The months to come would later be a blur, trying to forget emotions I didn't know could be felt. As time went on I saw the bigger picture.

All of Dustin's belongings were here with his family in Sedona. Everything was packed up. My mom and I didn't have to go to his house, go through his things and pack everything, that would have been emotionally difficult. We had to power through a challenging time. It's so strange how the universe works.

Dustin was all I had in Los Angeles. If we hadn't moved to Sedona together there is no way I would have stayed in Los Angeles. I would have had to quit my job, pack up my belongings and relocate. All of those things are hard anyway, I couldn't have imagined doing those things while grieving the loss of my brother. Having to find a new job, that would have been very difficult. Instead, I had already relocated to where my family was. I already had a job that allowed me to take several weeks off. I had huge amounts of support from my employer and my co-workers as well as support from friends in the community. I was already settled into my home and near my family.

My family brought my brother home. Dustin was set free in Sedona, a place that he loved—the place he always called home. I took some of his ashes up in the airplane above Sedona. We finally got to do our skydive together. I set him free while free falling from 10,000 feet above paradise. Once I touched down on the ground I looked up. All of the spectators along with all of my family and friends were in awe at what was happening.

The ashes I released in free fall immediately began to take on a life of their own. The ashes clustered, not quite ready to fully release, and began to form a heart.

Dustin had returned home . . . as I did too.

CHAPTER NINETEEN
Journey of 10,000 Miles

Loretta Jane Hido was born and raised in McKean, PA, a small town outside of Erie. She is from a big family with seven siblings. Her passions include photography, hiking, traveling and dancing. She lives in a cabin by the creek, the Hido-Way. Loretta is 51 and has lived in Sedona for sixteen years.

Father's Day weekend! All eight children were headed home to see our dad. He had worked two jobs to support his beautiful bubbly wife and eight children—six lovely girls and two boys. We lived out in the country on a dirt road across from horses and cows.

In his youth my dad was planning to be a pitcher for the Pittsburgh Pirates, but that all changed and off to war he headed right after high school. He was in World War II and the fight continued his whole life. Raising eight kids was no picnic, that I can assure you! My dad worked as a foreman for GE until he retired. On the weekends he was a Pennsylvania Game Warden.

Shortly after his retirement, my dad began to lose weight. He said he wasn't as hungry anymore. Since he was retired he was always keeping busy doing things around the house and our big yard. Shortly after that, in March of 1996, we got our father to go to the hospital for some tests. The results weren't good.

Dad had a tumor that engulfed his whole stomach. No wonder he wasn't hungry. His stomach was barely large enough for food to pass through. The tumor was strangling his desire to eat. They told us there was no cure. Radiation was started, but the outlook was grim. He continued to wither away.

It was Friday, June 14th, Flag Day, 1996. Flags were flying

everywhere I remember. We knew it was near the end for my father because hospice had come and was trying to help him through the pain and suffering of his life coming to an end. He stayed strong through it all and never complained. He never wanted us to worry about him.

All eight kids were headed home that Friday, as Sunday of all things was Father's Day! Seven of us made it home on that Friday and my little sister was almost home—about four hours away—when my dad was rushed to the ER with an infection. He was nearing his death.

As the seven kids and my mom were at the hospital waiting for my dad to get his care and some medicine to help him through the night, we had to step out of his ER for a few minutes by request of the doctor.

All of a sudden over the hospital loud speakers we heard the awful words: *Code Blue! Code Blue!* Within minutes his room was flooded with doctors, nurses, techs, we didn't even know who else. It was all a blur.

As the curtain was opened we could see what seemed to be the violent pounding on his chest and machines and all this drama going on. His heart had given out. My dad was a 'Do Not Resuscitate,' but I'm sure with the family all standing by, they wanted to try to save him . . . for us . . . for him . . . for Father's Day.

But, this didn't happen. My father died that night in the ER. They had us all say our goodbyes and we left the hospital room in a fog. You know the end is near, but until it actually happens, you have no idea of the pain, sorrow and heartbreak one will have to endure after losing a parent like this. We made the call to my little sister not to rush coming home. She was still on the interstate racing to make it to the hospital.

Father's Day we shared together. My mother and all eight children, all of us crying, all of us sharing stories and making plans for his funeral. The hospice doctor and nurses came to our aid. They came to our country home and spent the day with us. My mom continued to cook her homemade Sunday dinner, but we all could barely eat. We were sick inside.

Most of his Father's Day gifts he enjoyed before he passed. We put them in his casket. The lines coming in to his showing were unexpected. The funeral director said he had never seen such lines of people coming in to support a family like this. We were so overwhelmed at the outpouring that came to say their last goodbyes to my dad and to share this moment with us. I took it really hard. It's difficult to watch someone you love and respect and admire wither away to nothing and then you watch him suffer and die. It was my wake-up call.

So, being a middle child and being so pained inside, confused and upset (like why do bad things happen to good people?), I gave 30 days' notice at my job that I had been at for about eight years. I bought a big map of the U.S. I'm going on a road trip and I'm going to see the places and things I'd always read about or heard about. I'm going to take a journey . . . I'm going to live . . . I'm going to heal!

On the map I highlighted places like Mount Rushmore, Branson, Yellowstone, Salt Lake City, Reno, Lake Tahoe, Las Vegas, Four Corners, Grand Canyon, Phoenix. Off I went! I was determined to make my dad's passing a motivation to live.

I left my small home town of McKean and went all the way to California, down and around, going 10,000+ miles and hitting 21 states. Driving, driving, driving . . . photographing, hiking, thinking and trying to heal.

While driving from Las Vegas heading to Phoenix, I took a wrong turn. In retrospect, I now know it was the 'right' turn. I was off the beaten path on Highway 89 South headed toward Prescott when I saw a little sign reading, 'Sedona.' I thought, *Hmmm. Didn't I once hear about someone saying if you are ever in Arizona, stop in Sedona? Hmmm. Why? What's there?* I pondered.

Oh well, I was heading toward this place—Sedona. I didn't know why. I didn't know what was there. Heck, it wasn't even on my map! Oh well, off I went. Up and over the mountain and through Jerome. It was dark. The roads were scary. I saw nothing but stars as I drove up and over and down into Cottonwood and ventured into Sedona on 89A. It was almost 11:00 p.m. I saw nothing in Sedona! In fact, I didn't even know I was in Sedona! It was too pitched black! It looked like a small quiet place wherever I was.

While I saw almost nothing, I did see a sign for Hwy 179 that lead to the Interstate so I figured I'd get back on track and head south on Interstate 17 to Phoenix. I stopped at the gas station at the 'Y' on 89A to fill up. The 'Y' was what the gas station guy called the main intersection of Highways 179 and 89A.

I then got in my Bronco and realized I had no brakes! I pushed the pedal to the floor! Holy Moly! I had to stop wherever I was! There were no options.

As I was looking under the Bronco, an elderly man came from nowhere.

"Say Miss, are you having a problem with your car?"

"It appears I have no brakes!" I explained.

He started checking the Bronco for me and said, "You're not going anywhere tonight, lady, you have no brakes!"

"Where am I?" I asked. "Is there any place to stay here?"

"Ma'am, you're in Sedona."

He laughed and made a few phone calls and got me a place to stay at a bed and breakfast in town. He had me follow him and told me how to handle the emergency brake as I drove and that in the morning he'd get me to the tire place and get me settled up with new brakes, and he'd make sure I would be taken care of.

I asked him if he worked at the gas station. "No ma'am," he said. "I'm jes' a local."

I followed him to where I would spend the night. The next morning he came and got me and we went to the tire place, and he made sure the guys took good care of me. My Bronco got fixed up right with new brakes.

As my head cleared, I was in awe with what I was seeing in this most wondrous place! I'm like, *Where am I? What is this place?*

I ended up staying a few days embraced in this beauty. I hiked. I had my vortex experience! And suddenly I just knew this was my new home! This is where I would heal. This felt good. This felt right. This is where I was meant to be. This is where the Universe and God had stopped me!

I finished my trip across the United States—21 states, 10,000+ miles. I left Pennsylvania in October of 1996. Left my mother, all my sisters and brothers and nieces and nephews and friends. I left my whole life to start anew and to heal in Sedona.

POSTSCRIPT: I've been here since 1996 and my spiritual journey never ended. Every day I wake up and just think to myself, *Wow! What a place! Mother Nature at her best! God's country. Red Rock Country. Sedona, Arizona!*

And it only took 10,000 miles to get here!

CHAPTER TWENTY
Thelma and Louise

Stacy Moore is a transplanted Floridian native. She's been a newspaper reporter, public relations specialist, business owner and now works part time at Grand Canyon Harley Davidson. She loves to play tennis, write, hike, bike, swim and enjoy all the many wonders Sedona has to offer. Stacy is 55 and has been a resident for five years.

'Red Rock Fever' (crazy about Sedona) hit me in 2007. That was a big year for me in many ways. I was recovering from a devastating injury, did my first triathlon, turned 50 years old and made a major life change—I fell in love with a woman!

The year before on a girl's trip to the Grand Canyon I fell in love with Claudette. The problem was I was married to my high school sweetheart, the perfect man, and I fell in love with the perfect woman. It was a tough time for all involved and many heart-wrenching moments had to be endured.

Shortly after that revelation, I totally ruptured my Achilles tendon and went through a demanding rehabilitation. I entered my first triathlon eight months later and placed fifth in my age group! Ya-hoo!

Claudette and I knew we wanted to move away from Florida where we were living. There was too much drama from friends once we became a couple. Since Claudette's mom had recently passed away, there wasn't anything really keeping us there.

I had always been intrigued with the Southwest and Arizona in particular. I had stayed in a timeshare twice in Sedona and there was something about it that was drawing me back. Maybe because Claudette and I fell in love in the Grand Canyon, I don't know, but my fascination with Sedona could not be dismissed.

Claudette and I had already stayed in Sedona with two friends the previous summer and that was probably when we first were smitten with it. How could anyone not be? The glorious sunsets that turn the rocks fifty different shades of red and gold . . . the hikes into the wilderness . . . the star-studded skies at night . . . the small town feel. It all was there.

So we made a day trip back in May 2007, when we came out to Scottsdale to stay in a timeshare. We had a fun-filled day, but going to the Chapel took our breath away with its beauty and tranquility, not to mention the amazing views of the different red rock formations. We lingered there writing our commitment vows to each other, then to Heartline Café to enjoy our favorite meal—pecan-crusted rainbow trout.

We tried to find Cathedral Rock to do our ring exchange, but forgot that it was nestled in a neighborhood and couldn't find it. We ended up at Bell Rock, which was a good second choice, where we toasted each other and our love with a bottle of champagne. After that trip, I spent hours on the computer perusing house rentals, especially on craigslist. I remember my daughter found an amazing rental one time on it.

"You seem glued to that computer," Claudette would comment to me almost on a daily basis. "Still looking for that perfect house in Sedona?"

"Yes I am and I'm not giving up!" I'd reply with a smile and continue my hunt.

I loved the small town appeal of Sedona. There were no big chain stores and few street lights so the black skies were filled with twinkling stars that seemed so close you could pick them out of the sky.

After making countless phone calls, looking at what seemed like a thousand pictures and listings, I found 'the one.' The people who owned it sounded nice on the phone and the pictures with the outstanding red rock views pretty much sold me. And they were willing to give us a deal if we would pay the year's rent up front.

What did we have to lose, except a year of our life? To me it was a no-brainer. I just had to make sure Claudette was okay with it. I knew she'd miss her family tremendously. She and her sister were super close and she adored her little niece.

We both felt Claudette's mom's passing was a sign for us to move away from Orlando. We had signed a contract to buy a townhouse in Orlando just days before she died, but we were able to get out of it. Things happen for a reason. Even a week later would have sealed the deal and that's where we would be right now. Stuck in a rut.

"Claudette, I think I found our Sedona home," I said excitedly one day as she walked in the door from work.

"Let's take a look at it," Claudette said. She looked over the pictures and the price. "If you feel strongly about it, then let's do it," she said with a smile on her face.

And just like that we were moving to Sedona! To a house we had never physically seen. To a town we really didn't know. To a place with no friends or family to give us support. And neither of us had a job awaiting us when we got there.

It wasn't like we were twenty-something year olds fresh out of college with the world at our feet beckoning to be discovered. We were freaking 50 year-old women! I knew all our friends would think we'd gone crazy. My friends already thought I was nuts, leaving my husband of almost thirty years for a woman! This would make me certifiable in their eyes.

Who in their right mind would make a crazy move cross country? More importantly, what would our families think? How would my kids react? And my husband? Moving out of the house I had shared with him and moving into an apartment a few miles away is a far cry from moving 2,500 miles away.

A year lease is a big commitment. What if we got out there and hated it? Claudette's favorite saying is, "The greatest risk is not taking one." Well, we were going for it! It seemed so right just like everything else we had done together.

We all go through a lot of new beginnings during our lifetime. Being born, getting our first teeth, sampling our first real food, taking our first steps, speaking our first words, going to our first day of school, falling in love and making love—our beginnings are endless. Claudette and I were going through a new beginning together.

The house was available in August. We were already in the middle of June. We had a lot to pull together in a month and a half. We had two cars and a U-Haul to take cross country. Fortunately, we had two good friends who volunteered to make the journey with us and we turned it into a fun road trip. Thank God for good friends!

The biggest hurdle I faced was telling my husband, Don. I didn't want to keep this from him like I did my affair with Claudette. I knew it wouldn't be easy. This talk would be planned unlike when I told him about Claudette and me.

I used to go over to my house at some point every day from my apartment. A lot of times, Don would be there and I would call him on my way and he would have a cup of tea waiting for me if it was in the morning.

The morning I was going to tell him was no different. A steaming cup of tea was waiting for me. It always pulled at my heartstrings when he did this. I knew he still loved me and it hurt me knowing I was hurting him.

I sipped my tea, then looked at him. I took a deep breath. It's now or never.

"Um, Don, I've got some news to share with you," I began.

His eyebrows arched up and he looked expectantly at me and I'm sure he was hoping to hear something other than what I was about to hit him with.

"Claudette and I have decided to move to Sedona. We found a house to rent on craigslist and they gave us a great deal if we paid a year's rent up front."

His shoulders sagged. I could see the sadness written on his face and in his eyes. I just sucker punched him one more time. This was a more permanent move than just living down the street in an apartment. I know he thought that would be short-lived and I'd be moving back in with him where 'I rightfully belonged.'

And there it was. It was done. I was moving to Sedona with Claudette. I had never truly ever been on my own my whole life. Yes, I was away for college, but I basically moved from my parent's house to being married and living with my husband. I was always accountable to or for someone. Always. And now in my mid-life boomer years, I was about to be on my own. Frankly, it was exhilarating.

For some strange reason, I wasn't afraid. I had Claudette by my side and I believed in the strength of our relationship. Together we would make it.

We started telling our friends about our impending move to Sedona. I think a lot of them just shook their heads and thought we would be back—tail between our legs—before too long. We chose not to listen to the naysayers and looked at this as an adventure, kind of like *Thelma and Louise,* except we had no intention of driving off a cliff in the Grand Canyon!

It was going to be quite the change. Claudette had been a tennis professional her whole life, but she was burned out. So not only were we moving to a new place, she'd have to change gears and start a new career, and I'd have to go back to work, something I had not done in more than ten years when I owned my own business.

Time passed quickly. Friends gave us a farewell party, we said our goodbyes and we were on the road to our new life in Sedona. The days were long, but we had fun along the way. The owners of our proposed new home in Sedona were going to have their realtor meet us to give us the keys and go over everything. We gave him a call when we were an hour or so away. We ended up getting there before him and walked all around the house, peering into windows. Our friends were a few hours behind us.

From the outside everything looked fine, but when the realtor opened the front door—whoa baby!—a wave of stale smoke hit us like a two-by-four!

Claudette and I looked at each other with disgust. They must have been smokers. Why didn't we think to ask? And even though it was early evening, the house seemed dark and closed in. What had we done? Had we made a major mistake picking a house sight unseen and going by pictures on the Internet?

We glumly signed the paperwork and handed over our rent check for the year. For better or for worse, this was going to be our home.

"What do you think?" I asked when we were alone.

"It's going to be fine!" Claudette, ever the optimist, said. "We'll just open all the windows and air it out."

She was right. Our friends thought the house was great and once we unpacked and added our personal touches to it, the house brightened and it became a home. It was our Sedona home sweet home. Our adventure in the Red Rocks was just beginning.

Claudette and I had finally finished unpacking boxes, our friends returned to Florida, and we were getting somewhat organized. We'd been in Sedona for twelve days, now we needed to take a break and get out of the house. We went and had a bagel for breakfast at a deli in West Sedona and bought the local newspaper.

Sipping my tea and taking bites of my bagel, I perused the Help Wanted section of the paper. I nearly choked on my tea when I spotted an ad for Harley Davidson in Uptown Sedona. They were looking for full and part time workers! I remember telling Claudette the year before when we were visiting Sedona how I would love to work at the Harley store. And now here was my chance.

I was suddenly nervous. When was the last time I had a job interview? It had to be at least twenty-six years ago when I interviewed and subsequently got a public relations job in a Chicago area hospital. But that was then and this was now. I was a young 24 year-old with the world at my feet and now I was a 50 year-old housewife looking for a semi-retirement job.

I called. They answered. I inquired about the job. They said come in! Claudette gave me a peck on the lips and off I went. I didn't have a résumé or anything. I was just going to go in and sell myself. I was early and sat in my car gathering my thoughts and courage.

Come on Stacy, you've worked at newspapers and have done public relations. You've owned your own million dollar business and have traveled the world. This is a retail sales associate position, not even a manager's position. Just be you!

With that, I got out of my car and made my way to the store. The girl behind the counter went to the back and a moment later a woman who looked around my age came out. She had short brown hair and looked pleasant enough.

"Hi, I'm Mary, come on back," she said with a smile. She was soft-spoken.

I followed her to the back and sat in a chair next to her desk.

"Here, fill out this application and then I'll ask you a few questions," she said and handed me a form and a pen.

Mary asked me a few questions about my past jobs and then told me what the job would entail.

"When would you be able to start?" she asked after looking over my application.

"Anytime," I answered.

"Let's see, today is Friday," she said looking at her calendar. "How about coming in Monday? I'll put you on the schedule and you can work four or five hours to start with and then I'll give you more hours. You need to learn how to use the cash register and how we operate everything. Does that sound okay?"

I couldn't believe I got the job in less than two weeks! I had to tell Claudette. I was so excited! A few weeks later, Claudette got a job with Red Rock Jeep Tours. And from her postings at tennis courts, she had calls for lessons.

Here we were settled in our house thousands of miles from what was our prior home in Florida, we were happy and we both had jobs. Life was good in the Red Rocks.

Once we were more established in our Sedona home and in our jobs, we started looking at real estate listings. We had fallen in love with Sedona and wanted to make it our permanent home. The only times we had been in Sedona was the warm late spring and summer months so it was exciting to think about experiencing four seasons, something we didn't have in Florida. And we had lots of wildlife that wandered through our yard. We took pictures of javelinas, quail, roadrunners and even a bobcat.

Before our one-year lease was up, we started looking at several houses. Nothing worked out except the great realtor herself. She did her homework and came up with six houses for us to consider. We knew we were on the right track as we walked in the first house. Although it wasn't exactly what we were looking for, it had all the features we had asked her to find. The last house we looked at was on the outskirts of the Village of Oak Creek.

"This seems so far out of town," I remember saying to Claudette. But that was quickly forgotten as we drove up to the house. We both looked at each other. We knew without stepping a foot inside that we had found our dream house. We couldn't find a single thing wrong with it.

"This is it!" I said emphatically. "This is the perfect house!"

And it was.

POSTSCRIPT: We settled nicely into our beautiful home and are very lucky to have great neighbors and we've met many wonderful friends in the process. We're thankful every day to be living in Red Rock paradise. I have many customers that come into the Harley store and I always tell them how lucky I am to live in Sedona. I'm so passionate about its beauty and serenity. You can almost see the twinkle in their eye when I tell them I live here. It's all about new beginnings. If you believe, you can achieve!

CHAPTER TWENTY-ONE
Places in the Heart

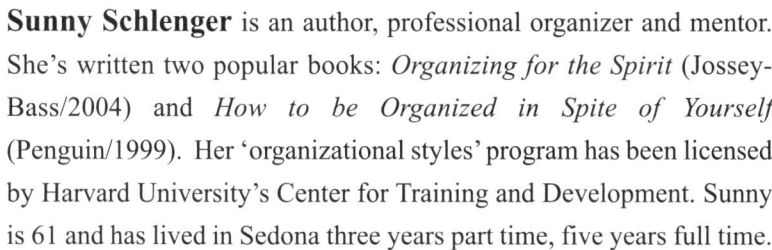 

Sunny Schlenger is an author, professional organizer and mentor. She's written two popular books: *Organizing for the Spirit* (Jossey-Bass/2004) and *How to be Organized in Spite of Yourself* (Penguin/1999). Her 'organizational styles' program has been licensed by Harvard University's Center for Training and Development. Sunny is 61 and has lived in Sedona three years part time, five years full time.

The year was 2004. My father had died a few months previously and my husband of one year and I realized that we had never taken our honeymoon. I told him that I had felt called to Sedona for some time and he agreed to come see it with me. Never having heard of the town before, he called it 'Sedonia.'

We arrived on a beautiful Monday afternoon with plans to leave the following Saturday, and were staying in a B&B below Thunder Mountain. Roy woke up early Tuesday morning and was out on the balcony when I woke up. He came back in and sat down on the edge of the bed. "I think I could live here," he announced.

"What? We haven't even been here 24 hours!" I replied. I thought I must still be dreaming.

"Really!" was his response. "I think I could."

"But you come from Long Island, NY and you surf! Have you noticed that there's no ocean around here?" I couldn't believe what I was hearing.

He just smiled and nodded his head.

That morning we took a guided tour around town and Roy casually asked the driver about land prices. I just stared at my husband, but later Roy mentioned that perhaps we could look at Sedona as a retirement community for the future. At the time we were both working—he as an air traffic controller at Kennedy Airport and I as a professional organizer and author. I said we could certainly think about it.

We continued our vacation with a visit to a spa, a trip to the Grand Canyon, a ride in a hot air balloon and on Thursday we rented a Harley. We stopped in a shop to buy a t-shirt for a friend and on the way out, Roy missed the turn back onto the highway. We found ourselves in the parking lot of a real estate agency.

He shrugged and asked me, "Since we're here, do you want to go in?"

"Why not," I figured, although I certainly hadn't planned on stopping at one.

We walked in and met the next realtor up, Amy. We said that we were just looking around at home availability and prices.

She asked, "Are you interested in West Sedona or the Village?"

"What's the Village?" we asked.

She then suggested that we take a ride to the Village, check it out, and meet her back at the agency afterwards. So we rode down breathtaking Highway 179 to the Village, took the first right turn when we got there, stopped and took in the view.

"Wow," we murmured to each other. "This feels like home!"

It struck us that this was a very odd thing to say. We went back to the agency and joined Amy in her car and headed back to the Village. She first took us to a house that was pretty much falling apart and inhabited by a few stoned hippie renters.

"No thanks," we said. "We'd really prefer something newer."

"Hmmmm . . ."

She looked over her listings and said that there was a newly built house that might or might not be under contract, but she'd take us to look at it anyway.

We pulled up in front and went in. The house was open and

spacious and interestingly enough had the same layout design as one we'd seen recently that we loved. Roy and I split up and headed through the house from opposite directions. When we were finished exploring we met up in the kitchen where Amy was waiting.

Roy looked at me and said, "Well, Sunny, do we need to look any further?"

I replied, "No, I don't think we do," and we both turned toward Amy who was staring at us with her mouth open.

"You want to buy this house?" she asked, looking back and forth from one of us to the other.

Somehow we were nodding and agreeing and asking her to check if it was available. It was, and we returned to Amy's office to discuss finances. I felt like I was in some kind of altered reality while Roy ran the numbers and assured me that we could do it. We could buy this house.

However, we had not come prepared to make a major life purchase and asked, laughing, "We don't have our checkbook. Do you take credit cards?"

The next two days were a blur of conversations with Amy and the mortgage banker she had us meet. Friday evening, getting ready to go out for our last dinner in Sedona, we stood on the balcony and Roy jokingly asked the Universe, "Oh Great Swami, if we're meant to do this, give us a sign!" I was videotaping the coming storm and darned if we didn't suddenly see three flashes of lightning in succession. We had received our sign.

We knew we'd have to go back home and try to explain how we'd gone away on our honeymoon and come back with a new house. People did think we were crazy, but our gut feeling was that we had done the right thing.

Fast forward a few years. We'd been using the Sedona house for vacations and were settled in quite nicely when my mother passed away. Roy was now eligible for retirement from the FAA and frankly was beginning to burn out from his job. The kids had left for college and there was nothing keeping us on the east coast any longer.

Roy said to me, "How about it, Sunny? New Jersey or Sedona? Sedona or New Jersey?"

It was time. I'm not a big one for change, but whatever had pulled me to Sedona in the first place was calling me back. I knew it was where I belonged. And because we decided to move when we did, we managed to sell our place in New Jersey right before the recession hit.

We moved here full time in 2007 and spent a few years thinking that we were 'retired.' Ha! Apparently it's been only the beginning of our second lives. We both began to volunteer and discovered passions that we didn't know we had. I've started writing again and am developing a new business partnership. I've met kindred spirits who I know are meant to be with me on this journey.

Back east was my place of birth, where I grew up and raised my family. But Sedona is our place of the heart. Whether we lived here during previous lives or just believe that we're meant to be here helping our community now, we know that this whole experience has certainly been mystical and much bigger than the two of us.